D1231658

SPIRIT OF AMERICA
Winning the World's Land Speed Record

SPIRIT OF AMERICA

Winning the
World's Land Speed Record

CRAIG
BREEDLOVE
with Bill Neely

HENRY REGNERY COMPANY • CHICAGO

*To Bill Lawler: who first gave me a lift toward the
world's land speed record and without whose
help and sympathetic understanding I never
would have become the world's land speed
record holder.*

Contents

1. Exit the Sky Kings   1
2. The Great Chicken Coop Caper   8
3. Saga of Saugus   16
4. El Mirage   27
5. It's Not a Moving Van, It's a Rubbish Truck   39
6. This Is No Hobby; It's a Business   50
7. The Case of the Gorgeous Model   65
8. Good-bye, Mr. Tuchen   77
9. Bonneville Revisited   84
10. The First Four Hundred   94
11. The Brothers Arfons   107
12. The Loud-Mouthed Kid Strikes Back   118
13. The Wildest Ride   123
14. It's Almost a Relief to Crash   133
15. The Rocket Car   153
16. Gunfight at the State Line Casino   160
17. Once More for the Women   168
18. That's the Spirit   176
19. King Without a Kingdom   186
20. Getting Going   205
    Craig Breedlove's Speed Records   214
    History of the Mile World's Land Speed Record   216

1.

Exit the Sky Kings

If I had grown up in Montana or Iowa or Texas, or *anyplace* else, for that matter, I don't know what I would have been. But I wouldn't have worked in an office and I wouldn't have done the same thing day in and day out, I'm sure of that. It would probably have been something creative, but I don't have any idea what.

The fact that I grew up in Los Angeles in a period when drag racing was also getting out of the toddling stage meant only one thing — I was going to be a race driver. I would build fantastically fast race cars in my backyard and collect trophies and giant sums of money and fame and make my family very proud of me. Racing was young, and so was I. This book is about how we both grew up.

My ninth birthday was a monumental occasion, for which I had impatiently waited. I got my first bicycle and, with it, the obsession for speed that has remained with me ever since. I gleefully wheeled the bike down the front porch steps that morning and out onto the sidewalk in search of the neighborhood kids — not to show off the gleaming chrome or white sidewall tires, but to show them how *fast* it would go. I hadn't even been on it, but I was convinced it would outrun any bike on the block. Three thousand skinned knees and 500 ripped shirts later I proved my point.

Kids used to see me coming and say, "Oh, no, here comes that Breedlove nut. All he ever wants to do is race."

When there was nobody left who would race with the "Blue Streak" (that's the name I had given my trusty racer), I had to find another form of competition: I turned to model airplanes and a neighborhood group of daring young men called the "Sky Kings." It was 1946 and the war was over, but it had left me with a tremendous interest in airplanes. That didn't completely stop the bike racing, though. I raced the Blue Streak to the club meetings—although now against *imaginary* opponents. I might add, however, that these ghostly competitors were usually world champion bike racers, and the crowd roared when the charming young American blew off the cream of the Continent.

The goal of the Sky Kings was to promote the design and building of airplanes—the gasoline-engined, U-control type—that showed originality, endurance, and outstanding flying characteristics. My goal, of course, was to fly *faster* than anybody else. With a goal different from the group's, of course, I had problems with the Sky Kings from the start.

I started with airplane kits, but when I had stacked a few of them up, I realized that I could compete a lot more cheaply if I started making my own planes.

The kits were really unsatisfactory for what I had in mind. I had already started to get interested in design and aerodynamics and could see many ways to improve the streamlining of the planes. However, as far as my parents were concerned, the thing had started to get out of hand. They had bought the kits, but they balked at the prospect of any additional expense. They knew, from hearing the other kids talk, that designing planes took lots of supplies and that it was pretty much a trial-and-error affair—mostly error.

It didn't take me long to get the message. The money would have to come from another source. Thus was born the Breedlove Airplane and Hedge Trimming Company.

I hopped on ol' Blue Streak and canvassed the block—the houses with hedges, that is. "I've got experience in trimming hedges," I would tell the owners, "and I think I could work you in on Wednesday morning. It would certainly improve the appearance of this beautiful place." They couldn't resist the big, soulful eyes and the cap and baggy knickers (I had seen the costume in a Jackie Cooper movie and it worked for him; so I dug deep in my closet and came up with a duplicate).

The hedge trimming gave me the money I needed, but I'm not sure that it produced quite the results my customers had in mind. When I wasn't sitting behind some hedge trying to work out an airplane design problem, I was cutting a hedge to resemble a series of wing sections. I had some explaining to do at times and didn't get too much repeat business. I had to expand into other neighborhoods.

The design business began to flourish in a corner of the tool shed in the backyard, and I bought all of the necessary supplies to start working on my own creations. I talked with some of the fellows at the club and learned that it would be a lot easier if I made aluminum templates for the wing ribs. This way I could then just hold the templates down on the balsa wood and cut around them. It was practically an assembly line project.

The fuselages of my new planes were four slabs of balsa with a long, streamlined profile. I accomplished this by glueing blocks of balsa around the engine opening and fairing them in to the smooth lines of the long, pointed propeller spinner. I could really streamline the body this way and was able to eliminate the canopy and all the other unnecessary stuff that increased air drag. I also had the only retractable landing gear of any of the club members. Well, actually it didn't retract—it fell out after take-off, but it was *designed* to do this and it did help to reduce the drag.

By the time I had six airplanes of my own design—Craig's Comet I through Craig's Comet VI—I was rapidly losing interest in the other end of the business, the hedge trimming. Yet simple economics told me that I would either have to cut expenses on the flying end or pick up the tempo on the working end.

I chose the former and began to perfect my flying technique: in other words, I worked on how to cut out the crashes. I practiced at slower speeds until I had all of the maneuvers down pat. Then it was back to flat out. I rigged the propeller so that it would come sideways on the compression, and I could bring it in on the belly without breaking the prop, since I didn't have any landing gear at that point. I also stopped adding planes to the model air force and started perfecting the design and trying to eliminate the problems on the existing ones. This cut the cost considerably.

My parents had been pretty patient with me, considering the fact that I had forsaken everything but the airplane caper and now spent all my nonschool hours in what I called the airplane shop, even though it was just the tool shed. I was living with my mother and stepfather and had a fairly happy home life—that is, I would have had a happy home life if I had ever come out of the shed in the back to take a look at it.

My stepfather owned a nursery a few miles from home and spent all day and most evenings with the business. It seemed that there was always some plant or other just coming into season and he was rushing around at the nursery pouring water on things and digging and whatever else it is you do at nurseries. I had never taken much interest in it because there wasn't anything fast about horticulture, and if there wasn't speed involved, well, I just wasn't interested. My mother had been a dancer in motion pictures when she was young, and she had had fast, fancy cars; so she understood my interest in speed a little better than my stepdad. If it hadn't been for her, I probably wouldn't have gotten to do any of the things I did. Before she had remarried, I was about all she had, and I guess she never did get over pampering me. I was always glad I had her in my corner, though.

My parents did feel, however, that I should have some interest other than airplanes, and they enrolled me in a private art class. Normally this would have interested me because I did well in art in school, but the class was held on Saturdays, the day the Sky Kings took part in the city-wide flying competition. I had won two trophies for stunt flying and one for design, so Saturday was about the most important day of the week to me. "Besides," I told myself, "who wants to sit around with a lot of girls and old ladies copying pictures out of magazines of horses and landscapes and things like that?"

So I would ditch art school and go fly planes. Some friends of my parents were supposed to pick me up on the corner of Sepulveda and Venice boulevards, and I would get there early, wait 20 minutes, and then go join the Sky Kings — after slipping in the back of the airplane factory and extracting the original Wheel-Dropping, Propeller-Saving Hedge-trimmer Special. When I got home, I would say, "You know, I waited 20

minutes for those people, and they never did show up;
so I went to fly airplanes." After a few weeks my folks
finally got the message. I dropped out of art school.

It was at about age 12 that my interest began to wane
in the airplane caper. I had the fastest planes in the
club, but there still wasn't a competition category for
speed. There wasn't even one for originality in
wheel-dropping or propeller conservation or any of the
interesting things. Just figure eights and loops and all
that stuff. I might as well be trimming hedges, I
thought.

It was at this point that a significant thing happened
in school. I was a good student and, despite my strong
outside interest, managed to make pretty good grades.
Fortunately the studies came easily, for I certainly
didn't spend too much time studying at home—that
time had been reserved for the planes. I guess I could
have been an honor student if I had just applied myself, but I didn't even pay too much attention in class.
If the subject didn't particularly interest me, I would
spend my time drawing airplanes or automobiles with
streamlined bodies. I've never been able to concentrate on things that don't completely fascinate me.

They used to show films at the Sky Kings meetings
about how air foils work and about a lot of other
aerodynamic design features, and I tried to apply these
principles in my classroom doodlings. One day when
the teacher started down my aisle, I covered my note-
book drawings and quickly turned to a page in my
social sciences textbook. There it was—a photograph of
John Cobb's land speed record car! The caption said
that Cobb, an Englishman, had set the record of 394
MPH on the Bonneville Salt Flats. "Wow," I thought,
"imagine—394 miles an hour."

"Craig," the teacher, who was now at my side, said, "*we're* not on that page."

"I know, Miss Johnson," I said. I also knew, in a flash, that I had found my goal in life: the world land speed record!

I went home that night and told my mother that I had decided on my life's career. She didn't say, "Yes, Craig, that's nice," or, "Okay, son, now go wash up," or anything like that. I think she somehow realized that this was not just a 12-year-old kid coming home and saying, "Mommy, I'm going to be a policeman." She knew deep inside that I meant it.

2. The Great Chicken Coop Caper

As the automobile phase began to grow on me, my folks gradually went out of their minds. For three years I had lived and breathed airplanes. The tool shed had been completely turned into an airplane factory and the tools were crammed into the garage — you couldn't even get into the car without stumbling over the lawn mower or a rake or something. Now I didn't even *go* out back anymore. I just sat in the front yard or gazed out of the den window and across the street to the Rourkes.

Roger and Gene Rourke, who were a few years older than I, belonged to a Culver City car club called the "Igniters," and their place was the unofficial club headquarters. There was always an assortment of fantastic street rods and chopped and channeled coupes in front of their house, and it was — well, it was paradise.

At first I would just sit and watch the activity from my vantage point across the street, but I couldn't stand it anymore. I had to have a closer view of some of that machinery, and I had to know what they were doing.

The first time I went over, there were parts all over the driveway and backyard. One of the guys was removing a transmission or an engine or installing some new piece of hot rod equipment. The place was just a maze of parts. And it was, as far as I was concerned, the real Garden of Eden.

Standing in the midst of the pistons and camshafts

and carburetors, I thought, "Man, this sure beats balsa wood and propellers." *This* was for me.

I went over to one of the guys and asked if I could help. He was in the final stage of adjusting a carburetor on a candy apple red '32 Ford coupe and I guess he showed remarkable restraint when he simply said, "Get out of the way, kid."

I was around a lot in the next few weeks, but there never seemed to be anything I could do. I was either in the way or too small.

The only way I was ever going to be accepted, I realized, was if I knew something about the mechanics of cars; so I went to the library and checked out an armload of books about the internal combustion engine and how it works. I *studied* at home for the first time in three years, and my parents were delighted. Their joy was short-lived, however. One evening my stepfather came up to my room to tell me how glad he was to see me taking an interest in my studies. He sat down on the side of the bed, and in his most eloquent father-and-son-talk manner said, "Craig, your mother and I are really proud of what you've been doing recently. I mean the studying and staying away from the planes and the guys across the street. You're really growing up."

He put his hand on my shoulder and said, "What subject are you studying now, son?"

"Engines," I said.

He looked at me in disbelief and asked, "What did you say?"

"I said 'engines.' Did you know that you can increase the displacement of a block by boring it and using oversized pistons?" I asked triumphantly.

He got up and ran out of the room shouting, "Portia, this kid isn't studying, he's reading about hot rods!"

A few days later I went back across the street. Armed

to the teeth with automotive knowledge, I went right up to Roger Rourke and said, "I know a lot about cars and engines and aerodynamics, and I'd like to help you and the guys with your cars." Somehow this colossal announcement failed to arouse much enthusiasm, and I found myself back in my own front yard.

My mother again came to my rescue, although she didn't realize she was doing it. She was talking to Mrs. Rourke one day and told her of the studying incident, because she thought it was kind of funny. I guess Mrs. Rourke must have been impressed by the fact that I had been interested enough to spend all those evenings studying about engines and all, and I think she said something to the boys — something subtle like, "Find something for Craig to do or get out of the backyard." Anyway, next evening after school Roger came over to the front yard where I was sitting with Flash, my dog (here was that speed thing again), and said, "Craig, I've been thinking, and I guess there might be a few things you could help us with. Why don't you come on over, and we'll see if we can find something for you to do. That is if you still want to help."

Did I want to help? It was about the greatest thing that had happened to me since I was sprung from art school. I beat both Roger and Flash across the street.

They did find a few things for me to do, although most of them were pretty messy, like packing wheel bearings and changing oil. My mother took a somewhat dim view of the operation on wash days. But I guess she rationalized that since I was just across the street and she could see me from the kitchen window — I was the super greasy kid lying under the '39 Merc — there was no harm in it.

Also when the fellows realized that I *did* know

something about cars and that I *was* interested in helping, they actually started accepting me. I was a kind of junior assistant apprentice Igniter, not just the kid from across the street whom they had to pamper or else find another place to work on their cars. Roger and Gene used to spend a lot of time explaining things to me. I knew many automotive principles, but now I was seeing the results of engine tuning and rebuilding firsthand. I really was interested and paid rapt attention to everything they told me. I continued reading books from the library on all phases of automotive construction and design and could sit and talk with the Igniters about anything relating to cars. They even took me for rides in their wild machines. I was the pride of the seventh grade — in my opinion, anyway.

Then one night, right after the fellows had come back from an Igniters meeting, the big surprise came. It was the moment for which men climb mountains and sail uncharted seas. They called me over and presented me with an aluminum car plaque. It read simply, but eloquently, "The Igniters, Honorary Member." I could have walked home on the electric wires, skipping easily from pole to pole.

By the end of my first apprentice year as an Igniter, I knew about all there was to know about building hot and classy cars: at least I had most of my classmates and my folks convinced of it. Actually, I had spent so much time *under* the cars that I had started to develop an upside-down view of motoring. But I was in the automobile thing *all* the way. I even carried a copy of *Hot Rod* magazine in my hip pocket at all times because it had become the bible of hot-rodders. I considered it a badge of the trade, and to be without one, I felt, was almost as unheard of as hanging around with the kids my own age.

It was inevitable that the day would come when I had to have my own car to work on. Much to the chagrin of my parents it came at age 13 — not 16 when I could drive it. Thirteen! They didn't actually say yes, but I started to haunt the used car lots in search of the perfect car. And I started to save money.

When relatives asked me what I wanted for Christmas or my birthday, I answered, "Money. No presents, just money." I got a job after school sanding cars in a body shop for 50 cents an hour. After four months, and with the help of a few sympathetic relatives who took me at my word at Christmas time, I had saved $45, and then the great discovery day came.

There it sat on a used car lot in Santa Monica — in all its rusty splendor — a '34 Ford three-window coupe. The only problem was that the price was $75, which left me roughly 30 hours of sanding, one birthday, and one Christmas short.

To say I had worked out the perfect pitch by the time I got home would be an understatement. This $30 I needed was really important. It represented a chance to make something of myself — a chance to make up for the first 13 years of my life, which at this stage I considered pretty much wasted. Everything hung in the balance, and Clarence Darrow never pleaded a case more magnificently. I stepped back to accept the plaudits of the adoring jurors and well-manneredly slipped back into the role of the perfect son, obediently awaiting the verdict.

My stepfather looked at me sternly, judgelike, and said, "All right, but it's going to represent your birthday present."

It was the greatest birthday present I had ever received, and it wasn't even my birthday. He quickly added: "And there will be no driving your car until you're old enough for your license."

I had already covered that point in my brilliant summation. It came right after the part that went something like: "And if allowed to get the car, I promise to obey the rules of the road, to keep myself physically strong, morally straight, and in bed by nine each night."

Actually I did realize that it would take many long months of hard work before the coupe would be ready to race — er, drive. If I had had any idea at that point just how many cars I would have to sand to get the money for parts, I might have waited longer — say ten or twenty minutes longer.

All autobiographies should have a sentence that goes something like: "This is where it all started." Well, this *was* where it all started. I could finally, at the ripe old age of 13, put into practice some of the things I had learned while pausing for about six thousand hours under the cars of *other* hot-rodders. You see, *I* was now a hot-rodder. The fact that I couldn't drive had nothing to do with it. I had a hot rod and, consequently, I was a hot-rodder — plain and simple.

I could make use of my considerable knowledge of aerodynamics and my firm grip on body work techniques (at least the car-sanding part). About the only facets of my 13 years of experience I didn't bring into play in my first few days of planning were the hedge-trimming period and my artistic ability, but they were to be of use later.

At first I worked on the car in the backyard, but that was fairly unsuccessful. I had to keep the parts covered all of the time, and it was a real problem. It rained a lot that first year. All of the fellows who worked in Roger's backyard were there only a few days and for relatively minor projects. This one of mine was going to last for three years, and there wasn't that much canvas in Los Angeles.

Thus began the search for drier and more elegant quarters in which to rebuild the coupe. I looked all over the Venice area and found that it's pretty tough for a 13-year-old to rent anything—not to mention someplace to build a *hot rod*. So when a school chum offered to let me use a chicken coop in his backyard, I accepted. Well, it was *drier,* and besides the price fit right into my budget. It was free.

With the help of a couple of the Igniters, I poured a concrete slab in the place and a three-year process of building a drag coupe began. Part by part, nickel by nickel, the car began to grow. First I pulled the '37 flathead engine (an earlier go-faster attempt of someone) and put two super-charged flatheads in it—one in the front and one in the back. Man, what a charger that would have been *if* someone hadn't broken into the place and stolen the rear engine—super-charger and all. I guess I could have called it the great chicken coop (coupe) caper if I had seen any humor in it. But it wasn't funny. I had sanded cars and run errands and saved for nearly a year to get the coupe to that stage, and the whole affair was pretty traumatic.

It took me a while to get over the robbery, but I found that if I spent even *more* time working after school and at night, I didn't think about it as much. Even at age 14 I was able to reason with myself and come up with pretty rational decisions. I knew that this concerted effort at car sanding and neighborhood chores would not only help me over my first real tough period, but would give me more money and get me back to work on the coupe sooner.

This was about the first time my stepdad felt that

some good might come out of the hot rod project. He told me that he was really proud of me for the mature way I had handled the whole affair, and he did one other thing. He offered to lend me some money if I wanted it. This was really important to me because I realized for the first time *myself* that I was beginning to grow up a little. "Thanks," I said, "but I want to work and make it myself." We were both proud of the decision I made.

The next months saw the coupe again become a
one-engined car, but what an engine. The pride of the
flathead brigade. And that was saying a lot in those
days because drag racing was still pretty much a
flathead affair. The overhead valves—at least the
V-8's—were a long way from dominating the racing
scene. As a matter of fact, the first 270 Jimmys,
(six-cylinder, 270-cubic-inch GMC truck engines that
were destined to dominate drag racing) were just starting to make the scene, but there were relatively few
competition parts, particularly super-chargers, for
them; so it was still a flathead world.

The backyard nature of the project didn't hamper
me, because all of the cars then were homemade creations. It was years later that the factory and automotive
part suppliers really got into the act. In those days it
was actually possible for a kid to get a part-time job
and, with meager proceeds, build a competitive drag
car. He didn't need the vast support of Ford or Chrys-
ler or GM or anybody. He could do it himself, and
kids all over Los Angeles and southern California *were*
doing it. I guess this is why people still think of southern California when someone mentions drag racing.
Drag racing was the fastest-growing sport in the nation,
and I was right in the middle of it— and was not far
from actually driving myself.

In fact, I *was* driving some. There was an alley right behind the chicken coop which was about two blocks long and looked like the perfect spot to test the coupe. The alley was fairly smooth, with sandy soil, and it dead-ended into a hillside. My folks gave me permission to test the car there if I didn't go too fast and if I promised not to get out on the street. It sounded like a fair deal; so I went to work in earnest to get the coupe ready to run. All of the custom body work and the interior and the refinements could come later. Right now I just wanted to *drive* that car.

I didn't need much coaching when the day for my first test drive came, because I had spent the last two years watching every gear shift and every turn of the wheel that the Igniters had made when they took me for rides. Despite my confidence, a couple of the fellows came up anyway when I told them the car was ready. We made a few final adjustments, and they told me over and over again just what to do. They were like a couple of teen-age fathers.

We pushed the car out of the garage (I had long since stopped calling it a chicken coop) and onto the alley, and I got in and sat there for a minute. I was about to drive *my* car. I wasn't even thinking of the bragging I would do next day to my classmates; I was just proud of what I had done. And I knew it was to be one of the most important drives of my life.

I started the engine, put the car in gear, and eased out on the clutch. I was moving, a little jerkily, but moving. I looked back at the dust the coupe was kicking up — at the fantastic speed of 25 MPH — and I just sat back and felt lucky.

I found lots of excuses to test the car after that, and I think it took me about two months before I could get back to working on the car seriously. I would tighten one bolt and then take the car out back to see how it performed. At least I was getting lots of driving practice.

The driving experience also produced a strong desire to see how it was done at speed, especially since I had long before talked the Rourke brothers into taking me to the Sunday Drag Strip meets. Fontana was the first drag strip in the area and one of the first in the nation—the mecca of speed-struck fans in southern California in the early 1950s. It was about 60 miles east of my house, and all of the fellows went there every weekend. I built up lots of time as a spectator at that track, but I was really there for more than just watching. I was learning from the mistakes and from the gambles that worked—the tricks of the trade. And I didn't forget a thing I saw. I filed it all neatly away in my racing library—the thing most people consider a brain. When that glorious sixteenth birthday finally came, I would be ready. So would the coupe.

Then Saugus Drag Strip opened and started a Saturday meet. It was pretty close to home, too; so we also started going there each week. This gave us an entire weekend of breathing exhaust fumes.

Bill Adair, one of the first drag racers to take me under his wing, had about the fastest dragster at Saugus. It was a super-charged rocket that ran on fuel, and this made it sort of exotic. Most of the cars ran on ordinary gasoline, but the really fast ones ran on this mixture of alcohol and nitro methane fuel. It wasn't just a simple matter of changing over from gasoline to fuel; the engines had to be designed to stand the added kick the fuel gave. They were the real crowd pleasers, the ones that went the fastest—the top eliminators.

Bill took me to Saugus one night and as we pulled

into the pits he said, "Want to run it down the strip, Craig? It's early, and there's not too much going on."

I sat there and looked at him. Was he really saying what I thought he was saying? Me? Drive a fueler? "Wow, would I!" I finally blurted out. He went over to the starter, and by the time he got back I was strapped in, helmet on and ready to go.

"Now, listen. Keep it straight and you won't get in trouble," he said. "Get off the accelerator when you get through the lights, and shut the engine off when you get it stopped. Go get'em, kid," he said.

I was only 15 — I don't even know if my parents know about the incident to this day — but there I was on the starting line at Saugus.

I'll never forget the thrill that accompanied that first run — the feeling in the pit of my stomach when I let the clutch out, tramped the accelerator, and felt the power pulling me down the racetrack. It made my chest throb and my fingers tingle. It was injecting the booster shot of racing fever in my veins. No more kid stuff — this was the real thing. I thought, "Will my six-teenth birthday *never* come?"

I had gone 127 MPH in my first run — at 15!

Bill smiled when I got back to the pits with the car and said, "That should shake up your friends at the drive-in." He was referring to the Clock Drive-in where I went often with my buddies from school.

Practically every evening we sat around at the drive-in, waiting for somebody we knew to ask us to get in his car. Someone usually did, and we would sit there for an hour or two, telling racing tales and talking about cars and girls. Bill was right. Tonight I *really* had something to tell them.

These were impressionable days for me and hardly a

week went by that didn't bring another "greatest thrill of my life."

The next in a long line of "greatest thrills" came when my folks allowed me to go to Bonneville in August for Speed Week with Bill and another Igniter, George Farrell. My folks really liked Bill and George and felt that they would watch out for me. In fact, they *had* been watching out for me since I was 12. It was also part of a deal I had made with my folks. They were still concerned that I hadn't shown more interest in school than I had, and they said they would let me go if I brought my grades up to a B average. I knew this wouldn't be too tough, and Bonneville was important enough for me to make even the *supreme* sacrifice – studying.

There was nothing as big in hot rodding as the Salt Flats at Bonneville. It had been the first place hot rods had competed, and it was still the fastest. I was about to go there.

Bill and George were taking a twin-engined roadster, which we towed up with George's '46 Ford business coupe. There were just the three of us, and I remember the Ford boiling everytime we tried to go over a mountain. At one point George was sitting on the front fender as Bill drove. He had a five gallon can of water and was mopping down the radiator to try to keep it cool.

Racing heroes in the early 1950s were an exciting blend of legend and reality, and I was really excited to be involved with two of the real giants of racing – even if one of them was sitting on the front fender of a boiling Ford and the other was swearing at it when it got so hot that it wouldn't run at all.

Here I was, a 15-year-old kid, with two race drivers, in their mid-20s, sharing all their problems and talking about racing and actually being part of the crew. Big names have always impressed me; even today I stop and stare in awe at a movie star or a famous sports hero. So you can imagine how I felt at 15.

The trip to Bonneville was a dream come true. When I wasn't sitting up front between Bill and George, I was curled up in the back of the car, sleeping on the luggage compartment just behind the front seat—the only seat those business coupes had. Bill and George talked a lot about what their strategy would be when they arrived at the Salt Flats and even asked my advice on a couple of points. I was about as well informed on hot-rodding as many of the older fellows, and this was something of which I was proud. I never tried to show off, though, and I think this is why the older guys accepted me and tried to help me, and why the kids my own age looked up to me.

When we arrived in Wendover, the closest town to the Salt Flats, it seemed that every hot-rodder on earth had invaded the town. Wendover is about six miles from the Flats and the only place where they could do any major work on their cars. They could do some minor repairs on the racecourse but most of the work had to be done in town because there was no electricity or anything else out on the Flats.

There were thousands of kids and hundreds of cars. It was a fantastic sight watching the cars running up and down the streets and seeing all of the racers, with parts literally strewn all over Wendover. We didn't even stop in town but went right to the Salt Flats and rolled out our sleeping bags. It was after midnight and it had been a long, tiring day, but trying to sleep was ridiculous. I was so excited I don't think I got more than an hour's sleep, and this was divided into about twelve equal parts.

When the sun came up I couldn't believe the sight.

Stretching out before me was the largest expanse of anything I had ever seen. I knew the Pacific Ocean was bigger, but at that moment I would have argued the point. Here was this huge mass of nothing but white. It looked like a giant frozen lake, and I guessed you could go about nine thousand miles an hour on it. Within 15 minutes after sunrise there were about 200 cars there with drivers who felt the same way and about 2,000 fans who were sure the cars were going that fast just warming up.

George went 179 in the roadster, and I couldn't have been happier if I had been behind the wheel myself. After all, I was an official crew member and I had a pit badge on my crew jacket to prove it. As I recall, I wore that jacket and badge to school almost every day for the rest of the year — even when I didn't need a jacket. The teachers weren't too wild about it, but the kids were.

The trip home did even more for my pride than the one to the Flats. I proudly shared the back of the car with this giant trophy that *I* had helped win. I had been a crew member on a Bonneville-winning car! We got to my place about one in the morning, but I wasn't satisfied until my folks — even Flash — had gotten up and seen the trophy. I think that in spite of the late hour they were a little proud of us, too.

The big trip had convinced me of one thing — I needed a better-paying job than the car sanding bit. I had seen some great cars up there, and I realized that it was going to be expensive if I expected to compete in *that* league. And with my sixteenth birthday only a few months away, there wasn't much time to get it. I talked with all of my hot rod buddies and finally found what I considered the perfect part-time job.

Quincy Automotive in Santa Monica was a speed shop, and some of the neatest cars in the area came in there for repair and custom work. There was an opening for a welder, and I knew a little about welding from watching other guys work. Quincy agreed to teach me the rest, and I went to work for a dollar an hour. I worked three hours after school and all day on Saturday, and the job gave me both the welding experience and ideas from other cars, in addition to the money that I needed to finish the coupe.

The coupe was pretty much completed mechanically, and all that was left was the custom body work and the interior; so I stepped up the program. I worked every night and Sunday on the car, applying my body shop and welding knowledge, and had it ready to paint in about three months. The fellows at Quincy agreed to paint the car for me and let me work off the bill. They also helped me with the interior by taking the seats down to Tijuana, Mexico, to have them reupholstered. Most of the fellows were having their upholstery work done there because it was cheaper and, in most cases, better. Quincy loaded mine on with three or four others and took them down for me.

The seats were back in about two weeks. Man, they were beautiful! They were rolled and pleated black leather and looked like they had come right out of a Rolls-Royce. I had finished rubbing out the new blue and white paint, and we slipped the seats in. The coupe was finished, and it was a magnificent piece of machinery!

Then the big day finally arrived. I was 16. In the next few weeks I put the final touches on the coupe and with the help of fellow Igniters (I was now a full-fledged member) tuned it to within three-sixteenths of its life.

The first thing I did then was to announce to my folks that the *car* was ready and *I* was ready and I was going to Saugus to race it.

When my stepfather said I couldn't race it, my heart

dropped. "That's what I built it for, to run it," I said.

He said, "Absolutely not. You spent about four or five hundred dollars on the engine alone and you're not going to take it up there and ruin it."

So I said, "Okay, I won't go," and that closed the conversation. And then I went.

I had been to the races hundreds of times and had been in the pits just about as often; so the environment itself was nothing new to me. Why, I had even driven a car there myself—not in competition, but I had driven one. None of this mattered a bit. The feeling I had when I drove that race car into the pits of the Saugus Drag Strip on April 18, 1953, was unexcelled in my years of racing experience. (Well, it *had* been four years.) I knew almost everybody in the pits from having been there with one Igniter or another. Now I was one of them and for a moment was the center of attention. I'm the king of Saugus, I thought.

Every time a new car showed up at the track all of the other drivers would come to look it over. I took it as a great tribute to Craig Breedlove, race driver. What they actually were doing was looking over the competition to see how difficult it was going to be to *beat*. Nevertheless, the thrill was there, as I'm sure it had been for each one of them.

George and Bill went with me and we stood in the pits, tinkering with the adjustments for the four-thousandth time that day, and waited. I grew more apprehensive with each minute, not from fear of hurting myself but from fear that I wouldn't win!

Finally the time came. They announced the B Class gas coupes, and the next thing I knew I was pulling the Ford to the line. I glanced over at the car on my right and it looked awesome. It was a jet black '37 Ford coupe and looked real mean. They call the starting light on a drag strip a Christmas tree light because it has a series of lights that flash for each lane, top to bottom. When it gets to the last light—the green one—you jump on the accelerator and hold it down until you get past the next set of timing lights. "That black Ford doesn't look like anything I ever associated with Christmas," I thought.

Then the light was green and the two coupes were screaming down the quarter-mile with white smoke pouring from the rear tires. It had all happened so fast I didn't even have time to be scared. My racing career was officially underway.

I beat the black coupe, and Bill and George just grabbed me and hugged me when I got out of the car. They didn't say anything. They just held on to me, because they knew how much winning meant to me. And besides, nobody really *needed* to say anything.

When I got to the starting line for the next heat, my competition was a fire engine red deuce (a '32 Ford coupe), but it didn't look as mean as the black coupe had. I guess I had started to acquire the confidence needed to be a successful race driver. It's important, I was to learn later, to know you're going to win. And I knew I would beat the deuce.

The light flashed green, and I slammed the accelerator pedal down with the style of a veteran and sizzled off to my second victory. There was only one plateau left before the coupe, which I had now started to think of as Blue Streak II, would be the fastest of the B Class gas coupes at Saugus.

The final race was a close one, but I flashed through the timing lights about half a highly chromed bumper ahead of a '33 coupe called the "Red Baron." The charming young American of bike racing fame had done it—and with no skinned knees or torn shirt.

I held the trophy tight when they presented it to me.

On the way home, my only concern was whether to give the trophy to one of the kids to keep for me until I found some way to break the news or to just burst in and plunk it on the mantle—and suffer the consequences. It didn't take me long to make up my mind. I had worked three years for that trophy, and I wasn't going to be without it for one minute.

I wasn't really a bad kid, but I was very headstrong. When I made up my mind to do something, that was it, and I didn't like to argue about it. So that's what happened when I went to Saugus.

When I got home, I walked in the house and handed my mother the trophy. She couldn't believe it, and even my stepfather was really excited about it, so much so that it took him about three minutes to realize what had happened.

"I thought I told you not to race the car," he said.

I had it all rehearsed. I said, "I know you told me not to go, but I wanted to go. That's what I built the car for; so I did go. Now I'm ready to accept my punishment."

For the life of me I don't know why, but he said: "Well, if you're going to race up there, at least you might as well win!"

4.   El Mirage

The trophy stood in a place of honor on the mantle and served as a constant reminder that there was gold in them thar California hills.

The next lure, however, was to come from the Utah hills.

I had been running the car every weekend and had picked up three more trophies at Saugus and one at Fontana, but I had begun to look for broader horizons — and that meant Bonneville. It was only April and the annual Bonneville meet was not until August, but I had already started to make my plans and to formulate my dreams. I could just see the Bonneville trophy standing with the others.

There was one major project I had to complete, though. My folks had really started to get upset about my school situation. I had trouble thinking of anything but racing, and for the first time my grades were starting to get pretty bad. I realized that I had to bring them up before the end of the year or it was going to be a rough summer. Again my practical nature took over, and I buckled down in the last six weeks of the term, finishing my junior year with the B average that would give me a summer of bliss — working in the hot rod shop and racing.

During the summer the job at Quincy blossomed into a real challenge. I was officially a welder on the

muffler rack, but my unofficial duties included driving
the parts truck, sweeping up, selling parts—whatever
needed doing. As an added benefit for being his man
Friday, Quincy sponsored the coupe. In a *limited* sort
of way he sponsored the coupe. He donated gaskets
and bolts and anything that wasn't expensive. I bought
the expensive stuff on a cost basis, which, often times,
represented my pay check for all of the other duties.

I used the company pickup to tow the car to the
drags, and when talk of Bonneville came, Quincy
offered to pay my expenses up to the Flats. At 16 this
made me feel like the most important race driver in the
world.

When the time came, the 700 mile trip to the Salt
Flats didn't seem quite as far as it had earlier, but
then we didn't have a boiling radiator to contend with
and I was pretty busy with that swaying race car trailing behind the truck. It's funny how quickly the picture had changed. It had been only a year since I had
gone up to the Flats with Bill and George and now it
was all my show. What a gas it would be to go back and
relive those experiences from my early days of racing.
I've often wondered if I was ever quite as happy with
the later accomplishments—the really big ones—as I
was with those first ones. I think you get jaded with
success. Oh, sure, I got many thrills later, but I'm not
sure they ever measured up to the thrill I felt when I
wheeled that race car onto the Salt Flats in 1954. I
suppose a baseball player gets the feeling when he
plays in his first World Series game—even after hundreds of regular season games—and I'm sure an actor
gets it in his first Broadway show. It's hard to explain.
It's a kind of mixture of fear and joy, and you don't
know whether to cry or just jump up and down and
shout. Whatever it is, I had it. It was the Series and

opening night all rolled up into one. The regular season was over and here was Bonneville. I hadn't had
any of these feelings the year before at the Flats. I
thought I had been excited as a crew member, but it
was nothing like this.

There were race cars just about as far as you could
see, and some of them were really super creations. I
had been impressed on my first trip, but now I had
something far more personal with which to compare
them — my coupe. I didn't know if I could really compete, but I sure was ready to try.

Two of the guys from Quincy's were with me, and
we tuned the coupe on the Flats and waited in line. It
took considerably longer than tuning took at Saugus or
Fontana because there were about ten million more
cars at Bonneville. I think that added a lot to the jittery
condition of my already jangled nerves. My time finally
came, and I drove the car out of the line and onto the
racecourse.

They use a five-mile course for the timed quarter-mile at the Salt Flats, and this made the course look
about as long to me as the Mississippi River. Beyond
the timing lights there is just infinity. The flats stretch
on forever. It is the same on either side. The salt goes
right over to the mountains, which are 10 or 20 miles
away. All of a sudden, I felt lonely. It was just me out
there and miles and miles of nothing but more miles
and miles.

The starter gave me a go sign; and I hit the accelerator hard. The coupe leaped out and roared down the
salt. It seemed like an eternity before I reached the
timing lights, and suddenly the car began missing badly. By the time I reached the lights, the coupe had
dropped off by 20 MPH. This wasn't exactly the lesson I
had intended to teach these veterans. I had gone 128

MPH, the seventh fastest time out of 28 cars. In the process I had bent three valves.

We pulled the cylinder heads and found that the clearance between them and the valves had been too close. The combination of the high-lift camshaft and the milled (ground-down) heads had caused the valves to hit the heads and bend. It had probably cost us a much better showing, because the car that won the class went only 137 and I was sure that I could have gone faster than that.

As we pulled away from the Flats, I took one last look at the machinery there — an objective look.

Some of the streamliners were works of art. I couldn't believe how anyone could do that much work on a car. They were starting to be professionally fabricated race cars — I realize that now. They had hand-formed aluminum bodies and dzeus fasteners and handmade tanks, and everything was safety wired. The fittings and the hoses and all the bits and pieces in them were so much nicer than any of the machinery we were running at regular drag strips that I just sat there, wide-eyed. Once I saw how race cars were really *supposed* to be built it made a lasting impression on me. From that moment on I vowed to do fantastic workmanship on my cars and make them, above all, really fine pieces of machinery — well engineered and well designed.

At that moment the future began to fit into place, and I think I raised my sights about eight notches. Later, when I was building the jet car, I realized that before you even start on a car like that you almost have the entire machine, every nut and bolt, every axle and every conceivable part of the car entirely worked out in your mind — every piece of the thing, every panel and how it's going to hook on, every tank and where you're going to put it, everything you're going to do. These early days in racing were important to help me formulate my future ideas.

When I got back, I delivered another big shock to my folks. I guess it was really more of a disappointment than a shock since they expected it. I announced that I was not going to college. I wanted to build race cars, and that was the only thing I was interested in. I suppose by then they had pretty much given up on trying to change my mind about racing. If they couldn't keep me in art school, how would they ever keep me in college?

My last year at Venice High School was really something. I think I had two periods of machine shop, one period of drafting, one period of phys ed, and one study hall— not exactly an academic curriculum, but it gave me plenty of time to pursue my real interest. And besides, I could do a lot of work on the coupe parts in machine shop. That was the year that a very curious thing happened to me: I fell in love. It wouldn't have been too curious to most guys my age, but I didn't think I had time for it to happen to *me*—what with the part-time job and racing. But it happened, nevertheless.

Marge Toombs was a classmate of mine, and I had dated her from time to time for the past year or so. All of a sudden she started showing up at the Clock Drive-in every evening, and I found myself spending more time talking with her than with the guys. That was really taking advantage of a guy, talking racing to him and all the time sitting there looking cute and smelling pretty.

Well, I was in love, and I would just have to work it into my schedule. It wasn't too difficult, because Marge went to Saugus and Fontana with me and we were always at the drive-in together. She never really seemed to be too excited about the races, however, and it bothered me. I felt that she was just going because I wanted her to, and this didn't seem to be the way it should be happening. I've always been concerned about forcing anybody to do anything.

After graduation I went to work full time at Quincy. Life seemed wonderful. I was working around zoomy cars all day long, dating Marge at night, and racing every weekend. All this was to quickly change.

As romance will have it, along came the next step — we got married and got a little apartment near the shop. The next thing was that we were going to have a baby. This news left me with mixed emotions. I have always liked kids, and the thought of having one of my own really excited me. On the other hand, it kind of goofed up most of my plans. I had felt that I didn't need to go to college because I was going to be a race driver. Now that I was married and had a child on the way I couldn't be the race driver I had wanted to be, and I didn't have the education to do much else. I was faced with a real dilemma. I had thought these things happened only in radio soap operas, but here it was, happening to me.

The job at Quincy would unfortunately have to go. I needed more money now and I started asking my friends again if they knew of any jobs. Gene Rourke told me that Sam Hanks, the great Indianapolis driver, was working for Bill Murphy Buick and he might know of something. I went to see Sam and, in my usual hero-worshiping manner, said, "Mr. Hanks, I'm a race driver and my wife is pregnant and I need a better job." That was about as straight as I could tell it.

Sam looked at me and smiled as he said, "I know the feeling, kid."

Well, it turned out that Sam *could* get me on at Bill Murphy's and I was a little happier with my situation. Not only did I make more money, but I was to be around the hottest driver at Indy—a guy who was holding down a good job *and* raising a family *and* racing successfully. Maybe I could find out how it was done. I'm not sure if the situation had much of a soothing effect on me at all. As a matter of fact, I think it rubbed a little salt into my own racing wounds. Here was this guy who had the world on a string. He came back from each USAC championship race a hero, and *I* wasn't getting anyplace.

One day I asked him just how he was able to keep all the parts of his life straight. He looked at me and said, "You have to take first things first, Craig. Get your financial situation worked out, make sure your family is taken care of, and *then* go racing."

I'm sure it was good advice, but I felt that there must be a short-cut someplace. If I followed Sam's words of wisdom it would take me roughly 86 years before I could even get near a race car. At $65 a week there wasn't much left after the financial situation and the family were in order. So I was right back where I started—right in the middle of *The Romance of Helen Trent*.

Then I made a fairly logical decision: I'd forget about racing for a while and concentrate on my job. So I put the coupe away. Maybe something would come along and I could race again. And it did—I was promoted to assistant manager of the get-ready department (I think Sam might have had something to do with it). Get-ready was the department that serviced new cars before delivery to the customers and being assistant manager was a pretty good job. Then, not much later, the manager of the department got sick and was given an early retirement. I was named manager and all of a sudden my salary almost doubled. It had all happened very quickly.

After Christine was born and Marge was back on her feet, I decided that it was time to get the coupe out of moth balls — where it had rested faithfully for what seemed an eternity. Actually it was only three and one-half months.

I installed an improved super-charger on the coupe and won a couple more trophies at Saugus and the new Santa Ana drag strip. Then I decided that the car was ready for another plateau — the El Mirage Dry Lake. I didn't plan to drive the car myself, however. The Dry Lake course was fast and dangerous, and I didn't feel that I had the experience to handle it. Several guys had been killed there, including one in a coupe. The car might be ready for El Mirage, but *I* wasn't.

El Mirage Dry Lake was just what the name implied. The racecourse there was second only to Bonneville in prestige and was a rough, sandy strip whittled out of the rocks and sand dunes of a section of the Mojave Desert. It was long and fast and tough.

The search for a driver for a new car belonging to a kid was tough, but Don Rackeman, who now is one of the editors of *Drag News*, agreed to drive for me. Off we went to the Dry Lake. Don was driving several cars at the time, and when we arrived, Lou Baney, who was president of a car club called the "Screw Drivers," stopped us. He said the Dry Lake's Association (he was also on the board of that) was cracking down on certain driving regulations and it was doubtful whether Don could drive the car. "He's driving too many cars, Craig, and they're going to cut it out," Lou said.

"What am I going to do? Drivers are hard to

find—especially for a kid with a new car. I've paid my fees and everything, Lou. What'll I do?" I asked.

I got the only logical answer in the book. "Drive it yourself, kid. It's your car and you know it better than anybody," Lou said.

Well, my heart almost stopped. I thought, "You've really put your foot in it now, race driver."

"Listen, just get in the car. When you get to the starting line, I'll okay your driving card. Tell them you want to make a practice run that doesn't count. If you don't like it, we'll look around and see if we can find someone else to drive it," Lou said. There wasn't much sense arguing with logic like that. I either did it or admitted that I was afraid to. I got in the car and pulled it to the starting line.

Lou made the necessary arrangements with the officials. Racing was considerably more informal in those days; there weren't safety checks and driving tests and all of the things that young drivers have to go through today. Lou just told the fellows at the timing stand, "Let the kid have a practice run." And, like it or not, there I was, about to take a practice run.

The course is a mile and one-third, and it's just dirt—slippery dirt. Some yellow traffic cones were set up so that you could tell where the course was, and someplace down the middle of that big dust bowl there was a measured timing trap. *Someplace* in the middle of that mess—you had to guess exactly where. I knew that the track was pretty loose and that it was going to be quite a ride.

I looked down the track and everything was kind of stretched out of proportion and unreal looking. Walt Disney must have gotten his idea for *Fantasia* from this place. I thought to myself, "If Disney ever wants to cast another star for *Dumbo*, I know where I can find the perfect one."

I had butterflies in my stomach and my knees were shaking. You know how it feels when your knees get to knocking and you can't get them stopped. Well, this was ol' fearless Craig Breedlove—the biggest bundle of nerves in the Western Hemisphere. But that was the last time my knees ever really shook. I was uneasy and concerned lots of times after that, but they never really shook again. I guess my knee shaking episode falls into the same category as the early thrills. It was just a great big scare and I guess I kind of outgrew it, too.

The course record at that time was held by a car driven by Don Rackeman, the guy who was supposed to drive for me. It was a GMC powered Chevrolet, and it had held the record at the Lake for about three years running—setting the last mark at 137 MPH. And here *I* sat. I figured, "Here goes," and pushed the button. Somehow I was able to keep the car going in the right groove, and by the time I got to the timing lights I was really moving. The car was full of dust, but I could see the yellow cones plainly, and, man, they were going by fast. I got to the end very quickly and wheeled the car around.

People were yelling pretty loud when I got back. On my first practice run the flathead had turned an unbelievable 141! Everybody just went nuts because they had considered Rackeman's Jimmy coupe almost unbeatable and here this punk kid had shaved four miles an hour off the record in his first run. I felt great and somewhere along the line, my knees had stopped shaking. I said, "Okay, this one will count."

Suddenly people had stopped everything they were doing and were watching *me*. All of the work had stopped on the cars, and people at the hot dog stands had paused. All eyes were on the punk kid. I liked the attention and particularly the bizarre nature of the whole scene. It was like one of my racing fantasies when I was nine or ten. All of this gave me confidence when I approached the starting line the second time.

Off I went in a cloud of dust, and the coupe roared down the course like a desert lion. The run was wilder than the first because I got going a little sideways for the last few hundred yards, but it was too late to back off then—I had to keep my accelerator foot down. Being sideways cost me a little time and I went only 139, but that was good enough to break the three-year stranglehold the Jimmy had had on the record.

Naturally I wasn't satisfied after having gone 141; so I announced that I would tune the coupe a little and "have another go at it." I changed the plugs and the carburetor jets and just happened to glance over toward the Jimmy coupe. They were swarming over it like a bunch of apes and I thought, "Oh, boy, here we go."

Nick Arias owned the car and between him and Don, they had about all the experience in the book. And the whole thing was quite a blow, to have the kid come in from out of nowhere and dust them off. They went 141 in the Jimmy and that really made me mad. Imagine, I had made two runs over this crumby course and already I felt like I owned it.

Well, the next time out I almost proved that I did. The coupe went 144 and the whole place went wild. Not to be outdone in the one-upmanship category, either, I decided to tune it some more and come back for another run. That just about did it. I think the guys with the Jimmy figured that I was completely nuts, and had decided to sit this one out. I changed the jets again and went 148. Don came over and said, "I don't care if we put dynamite in that Jimmy, it's not going to go 148."

I think I drove harder and pushed the car farther

mechanically than I ever had because I wanted that record. After the practice run I overcame my fear, and I wanted to prove something to myself. A lot of people later asked Lou Baney how a *kid* could beat the Jimmy and he told them, "The day finally came when parts and tuning and driving ability all ended up in one car, and it won."

That was really my first taste of winning big. And it was the last time I ever considered letting anyone else do the driving for me — none of that "leave the driving to us" stuff for me anymore. It was all my show from that moment on. Still, there were a *lot* of times in later years when I sat in jet cars and asked myself why I hadn't "taken a bus."

But I was never without this obsession for speed, this fantastic desire to win, that always made me push everything to its limit — cars, parts, and particularly records.

5.

It's Not a Moving Van, It's a Rubbish Truck

My family situation had started to resemble my studies in my junior year of high school. I needed to pay more attention or I was going to flunk out of the husband and father course. It was difficult to be a good husband and father with the racing thing. Weekends found me at the track while other fathers were taking their kids to the beach. My evenings were spent working either on the coupe or overtime at Murphy's to earn enough money to make ends meet.

So, when Marge told me she was pregnant again, I knew it was back to the help-wanted ads. I found a job in the material and process engineering department of Douglas Aircraft and started to devote more time to my family. We went on picnics and to an occasional drive-in movie, and after Norman was born, I even stayed home most evenings.

I was still racing as much as my budget and my conscience would allow, however. New drag strips were springing up all over southern California in 1957, and it was pretty easy to race any night I could swing it.

Fortunately, it wasn't quite as costly to race in those days as it is now. I mentioned before that it was pretty much a backyard affair. Well, it was somewhat of a junk yard affair, too. The only *new* parts we bought were those we couldn't find used someplace — things like supercharger parts or actual speed equipment that had come out of southern California and not Detroit. We were often able to buy even some used speed equipment. There always seemed to be someone throwing in the towel and making some sort of desperation move — like going to work.

It was a more casual scene then. Most of the guys *drove* their cars to the strip. Only once in a while could we find someone with a pickup truck and go first class. We just towed the car behind the truck. And I can remember towing the car through the desert to El Mirage — they were real fun times. We would tow the car and drive flat out. It would be hot — and I mean *hot* — and I would be driving along with the heel of my right foot resting on the accelerator — barefooted — with the other foot stuck out of the window in the breeze. It's quite a trick when you're going about 90 with the truck and the race car along all those dirt roads back in the desert.

We had some pretty narrow scrapes on those back roads, too. I remember one day when we were late getting out of L.A. and I was really making tracks in Bill Adair's truck with my race car behind. We must have been going 95 when we came to a little bridge over a dried-up creek. Not only was it narrow, but the road curved to the left just past the bridge. By the time we saw the bridge, it was too late to put on the brakes because the race car would have jackknifed and flipped us at that speed.

On the other side of the bridge and slightly to the right was a small grocery store and filling station, with a house trailer beside it. There was no choice, we would have to go between the pumps and the filling station and get the rig slowed down straight ahead in

the desert. As we got across the bridge and were headed for the tiny space between the pumps and the building, three people stepped out of the door. They saw
this truck and race car heading for them flat out and just
dove for anything that would give them protection from
the big crash.

We made it through the small opening and I eased
on the brakes. It must have taken a quarter of a mile to
get the truck slowed down safely, and we got to worry-
ing about the people at the store. We didn't know if we
had hit any of them, or if they had hurt themselves; so
we decided to go back.

The truck had a twin Smitty exhaust system and it
always *sounded* like it was going flat out; so when we
appeared from the other direction it seemed as if we
were trying to race through the pumps the other way.
The three dusty people were just extracting themselves
from beneath the trailer and behind the building when
they saw us coming. One of them screamed, "Here
they come again," and they all hit the dirt a second
time. We got to laughing so hard we almost hit the
bridge.

Everything was more informal about racing. It had a
long way to go before it was to reach today's spohistica-
tion. There were no trailers and fancy rigs at the tracks;
they came later. About the closet we ever came to a
trailer for towing the race car was the time we borrowed a rubbish truck from the father of one of the
fellows to haul an Igniter's roadster to Fontana. It was
quite a scene when we arrived at the track. There were
all these clowns and the roadster in the back of the
rubbish truck. I remember the fellow on the loudspeak-
er saying, "Look at those guys. That really shows
ingenuity, folks, hauling a race car in a moving van."

About that time somebody screamed, "It's not a moving van, it's a rubbish truck," and everybody at the track broke up.

It was a world of fun and flatheads and Jimmys, and the only way we ever competed with the GMC's was by using super-chargers, which were made only for our cars. Jimmys, in fact, most of the time were unbeatable, and they were a little bit mystical and magical with their overhead valves.

Those early drag racing days were definitely the good old days of racing, and they were rapidly disappearing. Racing was becoming more complicated. The competition was getting tougher, and everything was getting to be less fun and more complex.

For example, the fellows in the club and at the drag strips were all beginning to talk about belly tanks and more advanced drag cars. The belly tank lakester was made from a large fuel tank that had been attached to the belly of a P-38 in the late stages of World War II. The fuel tanks were available at surplus stores in the area and were big enough to mount a large V-8 engine inside and still have room for a driver. The tanks, of course, were very streamlined in design and offered a low drag profile for a racer body. They looked like a large bomb on wheels — which is what they were.

I was going right along with the sport, I guess, because I was getting more serious, too. The Rourke brothers were building a belly tank, and the next thing I knew I was in the garage in their backyard (the garage came with the advent of more complicated racing) looking over the plans. I got pretty involved, and before you could say "Bonneville Salt Flats" I was a partner and the driver. It worked out fine because they couldn't go to the Flats in August, and I could take the car.

Marge really hit the ceiling when I told her the news. I guess she had a right to. She was pregnant for the third time and could see how much time I was going to spend on the new project. I promised her that I would only devote a couple of nights a week to the belly tank, but she knew that I would never be able to live up to that promise. I knew also that it would be a pretty tough vow to keep; so I began to think of a job that would give me more time to spend with racing and still pay the bills at home.

A fireman friend of mine told me that the Costa Mesa Fire Department was giving civil service exams; so I took the test. I was told that if I passed the exam and wanted the job I would work about 13 days a month. The rest of the time was mine. I could devote it to the family and racing. It sounded ideal. While I was on duty, I would be able to work on the plans for race cars, for the fellows had a lot of time to read and do what they wanted to do while at the station in the evenings.

The results of the exam arrived on the same day as our third child, Dawn. I was a three-time father and a fireman at 21.

The job at the fire department *did* give me the time I needed for racing, but, as Marge had predicted, I was spending less and less time with the family. The belly tank project had gotten more complicated than I had expected and I was at the Rourkes almost every day I had off. I missed the kids, but I was so involved with the new car that I just couldn't quit.

The Rourke brothers had gotten a new Oldsmobile V-8 engine from a local dealer, and it was a gem. Thinking of the speeds that the super-light belly tank was going to go really turned me on. I *had* to drive that car at the Flats.

The car was finished about a lap and a half ahead of my marriage. I knew that I had better ask Marge to come with me to Bonneville or we were about all over. She wasn't too wild about the idea, but when I told her that we could leave the two girls with my mother and take Norman, she agreed. Norman was three and really liked races; so he would have a ball, I convinced her.

When we left for Bonneville, we were racing into another era. The belly tank was powered by an *overhead valve* V-8 Oldsmobile engine. The age of the flatheads and even the Jimmys was gone, and with it much of the fun—all of the rubbish trucks and used parts were now racing only in our memories.

I qualified the Olds-powered belly tank at a respectable 236 MPH but lost the clutch. It was decision time again. At that moment we had just enough money in our pockets for the trip home. It seemed such a waste to have come all this distance and to go home without even really competing. But the closest place for parts was 110 miles away, in Salt Lake City, and then there was the money thing. Marge thought about it for a long time and said, "Go ahead and get the clutch. We'll get home somehow."

We drove into Salt Lake and bought a Ford truck clutch, hoping it would be strong enough. When I left the garage, I counted my change. We had 38 *cents* to our name. Unfortunately the truck clutch didn't hold either, and we were through. I had missed the one thing I wanted most—membership in the exclusive 200 mile an hour club. But at least I had gone almost 240 in qualifications, and a lot of people had taken note of that. It would help with my car building and driving credentials in later years, and I really felt that I was on my way to far greater accomplishments.

But the situation at hand was a more pressing problem. How does one get from Bonneville to Los Angeles with 38 cents? We thought of everything short of knocking over a service station, and there was just no way of doing it. Then something happened that was to give my professional racing career its biggest boost. An old school buddy, Dick Faulkner, was there with his father-in-law, Ed Perkins, who owned Perkins Machine Company in L.A. Ed came over and said he thought we had a really fine car and was sure we would do well next time. Then he said, "I understand you're a little short of money." He handed me an Associated Credit Card and $20, which seemed like all the money in the world to me, and said, "It looks like you need a sponsor. Come and see me when you get home." I don't know where he got the idea that I needed a sponsor. There I was with a despondent wife, a screaming kid, a broken race car, and a pick-up truck, and, oh yes, 38 cents!

That was the beginning of my first real sponsorship and one of the most pleasant relationships of my racing career. I never forgot that gesture at the Flats—as a matter of fact, I've never forgotten any of the people who made racing possible for me.

Ed sponsored the coupe and the belly tank the next year and things were going well in racing—except that they weren't going any *place.* I was winning lots of trophies, but they were all for the same thing, week after week. I was on a treadmill.

I had been working for the fire department for about a year when I realized that if I was going to make it big in racing and get out of the situation I was in, I would have to get started. Otherwise I would end up in the same boat as most of the other guys in the fire department—trapped.

I can remember clearly the night of the great decision. I was out at Station Two; we had gotten the place all cleaned up, had dinner, and were sitting in the little living room area, just Ray Gallagher and myself. I sat there and looked at Ray. He was about 50 at the time and I was 22. He was reading the fireman's manual on knot tying, and I could almost see myself in the same position 28 years later. It wasn't for me! It was the best job I had ever had, but I knew that I had to make the big move. That move could only be in one direction—the world's land speed record.

My entire life had been built around running at drag races and Bonneville. I was sure that my real future lay in the direction of the *big* record. To try to make it in oval track racing would mean that I would have to start at the very bottom and scrounge through for years and years with low purses and high travel expenses. With a wife and three kids, that was completely out of the question, especially when there was a golden opportunity just sitting there on the Salt Flats.

Mickey Thompson was one of the hottest drag racers around and was heavily involved in speed runs with his four-engine *Challenger*. He was getting a lot of publicity, which, I guess, started me thinking about the land speed record again. This LSR thing had been in the back of my mind since grade school days. I hadn't allowed myself to dwell on it too much when I was actually up there at the Flats because I was always pretty well wrapped up in the project at hand—either the coupe or the belly tank. Now I let my mind take the ball and run with it—and run it did.

The record had been away from the United States for something like 34 years—I remembered *that* from the seventh grade.

Now Mickey was running, and even though there was some doubt that he would break the record, he was running in the high 300s. Before, it had been pretty inconceivable to me that I could reach that pinnacle of hot rodding. There were no finances, and I really had nothing; I was just a kid with a dream. But Mickey demonstrated one very significant change, one thing that made the idea a lot more conceivable: Mickey was doing it, and that meant it *could* be done. He was just another hot-rodder, a regular guy, but he had put a car together with four engines, and he was out there challenging them. John Cobb was some legendary figure from a seventh grade textbook. Mickey Thompson was real — one of us.

"Ray, I'm going to break the world's land speed record," I announced to my studious companion.

He looked up from his manual and said, "Sure, Craig. Now leave me alone, will you? I've gotta brush up on these knots."

That did it.

For the next few weeks I was the most studious person at the fire station, but I wasn't studying about knots and fire fighting techniques. I had gone to the library and checked out every book I could find on aerodynamics and had started designing a land speed record car. There were drawings every place, and the fellows lived in constant fear that the chief would come over some night and fire me. We were supposed to spend a certain amount of time each day studying the fireman's manual, but I just didn't have time for that.

I remember one night when I was right in the middle of a particularly interesting chapter on the center of pressure in high speed aircraft design when the alarm sounded. I grabbed my coat and helmet and tucked the book under my arm. It turned out to be a fire in an electric motor of a warehouse air conditioning system and a couple of the fellows climbed up to disconnect the motor and put out the fire. It certainly didn't take all of us to do that. I guess I got pretty engrossed in the book while sitting at the curb under the street light, because the fellows got in the truck, turned around, and pulled it right up beside me and blew the siren. I went straight up in the air, and they broke up. "You guys won't think it's so funny when I come back to the station one of these days a celebrity," I said.

One of them piped up, "Sure, Mr. Celebrity, now would you give me your autograph so we can get back to the station?"

After weeks of studying and designing, I realized that the only engine capable of the speeds I needed was a jet. The piston engine had about reached its limit at both the Salt Flats and in airplanes. All of the new, fast planes were jets; so it stood to reason that the new, fast cars should be jets. Another factor was responsible for the jet decision: I had designed a slender, three-wheeled car, with the single wheel up front; and this needle-nosed configuration would lend itself perfectly to the shape of a jet engine.

I started haunting surplus stores on my days off and finally found a J-35 engine that had been used in a navy jet fighter. It had a $500 price tag on it.

It looked like the perfect engine, but there were two other small considerations. How would I pay for it, and where would I build the car once I got it? You just don't build a monster like this on the street. The car I had designed would be nearly 40 feet long. There was only one person, Ed Perkins. Ed had the *money* and the *space*.

"The conditions look just right to bring the land speed record back to the United States, Ed," I told him next day at his office. "There's a golden opportunity just sitting there." We talked the whole thing over pretty extensively.

I often talked things over with Ed. He was not only my sponsor but my friend. Mine were the only race cars he ever sponsored. He once told me that he did it because he liked me and enjoyed being at the races himself. He also said that he felt it was good for his son, who was younger than I, to see what was going on and that I was a good influence on him. Now I was about to pop the big question to him.

"With $10,000 I could get the design completed, buy the engine, and get enough material to get the thing off the ground and organized to the point that we could interest the big companies in it," I told him.

Ed said, "Okay, you've got it."

Enter, another era.

6.   This Is No Hobby; It's a Business

Ed had a place in his shop that wasn't being rented out—although it had been at one time. The mechanic who had worked there had left it in a horrible state. There was grease on the floor about two inches thick and the room was dark. It resembled a dungeon. Still, we needed a place to build this 40-foot-long monster, and this was obviously it; so I spent all my off-duty time from the fire department—15 or 16 days a month—getting the place in shape to start building the car. I scraped up the grease, painted the floor, walls and benches and everything that didn't move, and installed new lights.

Then, one day, when I had taken a few minutes off to get a haircut, I ran into an old drive-in buddy from high school days, Mike Freebairn. Mike was flying F-86s for the Air National Guard, and he asked me what *I* was doing. "I'm building a jet car," I told him.

"You're building *what?*" he asked.

I said, "Really, I'm building this jet race car, and I'm going to break the world's land speed record. I found a J-35 engine and we're gonna go very fast."

He asked me if I had ever thought of using a J-47. Then it all came out—the plans, the car, the fact that the J-35 was the only jet I could find, and that it seemed fine to me.

"Well," Mike said, "the 47 is from an F-86 fighter. It

puts out 5,000 pounds of thrust, compared to 3,500 for the 35, which is from an old navy jet, and the 47 is a much better engine. It only weighs about sixty pounds more, and it's almost exactly the same size. It's really a more advanced engine, Craig."

"Yes, but the 35 will do everything I need, so why add the extra thrust if I don't need it? I've read a lot about the 35, and it's a pretty reliable engine."

Mike pointed out that the 47 was even more reliable, and added, "It's newer than the 35, Craig, and they didn't bring it out just to have something to do. It's really much better than the 35. Just figure how much less of the total engine power you would have to use to go the same speed. You wouldn't have to operate at 100 percent power with the 47, and that's an advantage—less strain on the engine."

He had some pretty good points, and he was the first person I had ever talked with who had *firsthand* knowledge of jet engine performance. He had flown planes with both types of engines.

We went to lunch, and I began to get sold on the J-47. Then came the question, "Where do I find one?"

Mike was sure that the government had just sold a bunch of them as surplus and said that he would check through the Air National Guard. "In the meantime," he said, "come on out to the guard and meet some of the guys. I'm sure you're going to need some help on the engine anyway, and they would probably love to get in on it."

I did meet some of the guys and they were really excited about helping—so excited, in fact, that for starters they found the name of the company that had bought the engine. We went over to talk with the man at the surplus outlet and learned that he had been getting about $500 each out of them for scrap metal and that he had only one left. It was on loan to the Northrop Institute of Technology, but he could get it back anytime. The kids were using it as a training engine to take apart and put back together. This was great. We could actually look at the engine disassembled. For $500 I could buy a J-47 that I could see, part by part—no pig in a poke deal this one!

We went over to Northrop and talked with the instructor, who was delighted to help us. He said that the engine was completely disassembled and that the class would be glad to put it back together and run it for us. It would be an honor to be a part of the jet car program. Things were really rolling. Everybody I had talked with had been so helpful and enthusiastic that there was now little doubt in my mind that success was only a short step away.

Two days later the instructor from Northrop called and told me to come over. The class was ready to assemble the engine. I think I hung up the phone before I was in the coupe and on the way over, but I'm not sure. It may have been dangling from the table. When I got there, they were waiting for me.

All too few drivers care about such mundane things as what goes under the hood of their race car—or, in this case, what hangs on the back. They're mostly interested in how *fast* it will go. But I have always wanted to know *everything* about my cars, every nut and bolt that goes into them. So of course I wanted to see everything about "my" jet engine, too, and I was right there with the class, watching and asking the instructor questions.

I had called Bob Johnson, one of the jet engine experts from the air guard, and he arrived just about the time the class was ready to start; so I started picking his brain for some of the more specialized techniques. I was getting a short course on jet engines.

When the engine was assembled, they mounted it on the test stand and fired it up. What a tremendous sound! It started as a low hum and then rose to a high-pitched whine that made goose pimples pop out all over me. The whine changed to a roar, and I just fell back against the wall and yelled, "Wow." It was the sound of power, the sound of the land speed record!

Bob was impressed, too, but suggested that we take it over to his workshop and recheck it. "The kids may have missed something," he told me quietly.

We borrowed one of Ed's trucks and hauled the 47 out of Northrop, after promising to put one of the institute's decals someplace on the new car before it ran. It was there.

We found a few places where the kids had missed a safety wire or two, but generally they had done a pretty good job. I think it must have been a labor of love for them. I certainly considered them a part of the new team.

Anyway, I hauled the engine back to Ed's garage and went back to the drawing board, literally.

Things were moving so fast that I had forgotten one major item. I was working on some frame designs at the station one night when it hit me. "My God, I don't have any tires," I shouted. A couple of the fellows looked up from their reading, but they didn't say anything. They had gotten used to "the nutty kid" by then.

Tires were one of the most important items on the car, and I hadn't even *thought* about how I was going to get them. On all the previous cars I had worked on, tires were just an off-the-shelf item. But for an LSR car and the speeds that went with it, tires had to be designed and built by one of the major companies. There were only two companies that had any experience in LSR tires, Goodyear and Firestone. It would have to be one of them.

At that time Firestone was sponsoring Dr. Nathan Ostich in a jet car; so I figured Goodyear would be the one to contact. They were sponsoring Mickey, but they didn't have a jet car and I thought they might want to stay in the jet ball park and compete with Firestone. At least, this is what I told them in my letter.

This was all about as far from the neighborhood tire store approach as I could get. Here I was dealing directly with the world's largest rubber company. "Might as well start at the top," I told myself.

I wrote to Goodyear on March 23, 1960. I remember the date well. It was my twenty-third birthday, and I had stayed late at the fire station, composing the letter. Marge had asked me to be home early because the kids had a surprise for me, but I had forgotten.

When I got home, she didn't say too much. I think she had just gotten so fed up with racing that nothing much mattered anymore. She had helped the kids bake a cake for me, and they had been waiting two hours. I felt like the biggest heel in the world and I wished I could chuck the whole racing bit, but I knew I never could. I thought, "If she can just hold on until I break the land speed record, we can all go away for a while and finally get to know one another." But I knew that I *had* to break the record first, and I prayed that things at home would get better after I had done it.

After that night she didn't even ask when I went out if I was going racing or to Ed's place. She didn't care. The whole thing was preying on my mind a lot, but I still had commitments to Ed to race the car locally. At that point I certainly couldn't afford to let him down—that might mean the end of the whole jet car program. So I raced a little and spent the rest of my off-duty time working on the jet car plans.

About a week later I got a call from Akron saying that

one of the Goodyear racing tire engineers would be on the West Coast in two weeks and would stop by to see me. I really had to get moving. The plans had to be completed and I would need a model of the car and professional drawings and blueprints, and, well, just everything. So the car became almost a 24-hour-a-day project. Fortunately, I was able to spend some time working on the plans while on duty at the fire department, but even that didn't give me all the time I needed. The solution was simple: I would give up my sleeping time.

Art Russell, another buddy from my high school days, was working as a professional model builder for Revell Toy Company. He was the perfect one to help me with the first model of the car, but would he do it? Sure he will, I told myself. Nobody has turned me down yet. When I called him and explained the whole thing in detail, he said, "Yeah, it would be a gas." I was batting a thousand. I guess I realized for the first time how important friends are. Another benefit of growing up in southern California was that everybody was interested in racing, to one degree or another, and this really helped. As a matter of fact, it saved the whole project.

My next contact was to prove as valuable to me then and in later years as any I made. Mike told me to get in touch with a man named Walt Sheehan at Lockheed Aircraft. Mike had met Walt on an air guard project at Lockheed, and they had become friends. Walt had designed the air intake ducts for the Lockheed F-104 and could help with the same thing for the car, Mike thought.

Walt was very apprehensive when I contacted him, but he told me to come anyway. He didn't say, "I'll listen to your silly schemes since you're a friend of

Mike's," but that's what he meant. He was polite when I showed him the first drawings, but he started to get a little more interested when I told him the car had been designed with negative lift and incorporated some fairly sophisticated aerodynamic principles. Suddenly he didn't view the whole thing as a screw-ball plan by some kooky hot-rodder. He realized that I meant business and that a lot of thought had gone into the program.

Walt agreed to help with the design of the air intake ducts more as a challenge than anything else. This was a tremendous load off my mind. The ducts were one of the most important design considerations on the whole car. Fantastic amounts of air at enormous pressures were inhaled by the engine, and the ducts had to be (1) strong enough to hold up and (2) designed properly to get enough air in without significantly increasing the drag factor of the car.

Next stop was to see Bill Moore, a commercial artist and a good one. Bill was another of the fellows who had hung around with me at the drive-in; we had been friends since the fourth grade, so his name was the first to pop into mind when I thought of artwork to show Goodyear. I went over to his office and told him the whole story, and then I spread out my drawings. He looked at them and said, "What you want me to do is give you some finished artwork on the car, is that right?" He was right. He smiled and said, "Leave the drawings; I'll get started on it tomorrow. By the way," he added, "I assume you want the car to be blue, like everything else you've had." He was right again.

Nobody had gotten any money out of the project yet. All these people agreed to help out of friendship and speculation—mostly the former. True, I promised them all a real job once we had acquired a major sponsor and broke the record, but they would probably have done it without that.

Bill completed the drawings. They were tremendous. Man, what a great feeling I had when I actually saw the car for the first time — a full-color, highly professional rendering of my design. It made me feel great. I had done the original drawings, but they were just pen and ink. Here was something with highlights and color and, well, pizazz. It was *the car!*

Over at Art's house, we started on the model. I helped Art with some of the basic shaping and sanding (shades of the Sky Kings days) and he completed it. When the model was finished and painted and rubbed out, I just stood and looked at it, in much the same way I had looked at my kids when I saw *them* for the first time at the hospital. A new era of racing had been born in me. I reached down and picked the model up and rubbed my fingers over the smooth contours. I knew I was holding the new world's land speed record in my hands. I tried to count the thousands of manhours that had gone into the project just to get to that point, but I couldn't. Little did I realize that I was just getting started and that the big work still lay ahead of me.

By the time the Goodyear man got there, we had a great presentation worked out — complete with art work, blueprints, drawings, and the model. Walt Devinney, the engineer, arrived from Akron, and we put on a show that included everything but a seal act and four choruses of "Danny Boy" on tenor sax. As a matter of fact, we considered both but decided that we would save them for the big brass. We didn't need the extra acts anyway. He took one look at everything, politely listened to the pitch, and said, "Yes, I like it all. It looks great, and I'm going to recommend that Goodyear build tires for it."

I just sank into a chair and breathed the greatest sigh of relief yet. I didn't stay in the chair long, though, because I knew I had to keep pitching. The $10,000 wasn't going to last long, and I needed a major sponsor badly. I popped right up and said, "Great. We're going to make you proud of this car. Now will you ask the company if they can give us some financial assistance, too. We really need some funding. I think it would be a valuable asset to Goodyear's racing program."

This kind of startled him. Here was this brash kid who had asked for tires from his giant company — and then had the nerve to ask for money, too. But he pondered the request for a while and said, "I'll ask. That's all I can do."

It didn't take long to get a reply from Akron. Goodyear agreed to build tires for the car but said they didn't feel that they could put money into the project beyond that. It was a slight disappointment, but not too great. The tires were the important thing, and besides, with a name like Goodyear to toss around, other sponsors shouldn't be too hard to find. It should at least get somebody's attention.

I had the engine, the garage, $10,000 from Ed, a tire sponsor, an entourage of talent-laden friends. The project was really rolling. I felt that the logical step was to quit my job at the fire department and devote full time to the project. There were all these things to do and so many people had put so much faith in me that I felt it was up to me to produce. The only way I could do that was to give the car all my time. That's when things at home really started to fall apart.

That night I told Marge I had quit my job and was going to devote full time to the jet car. She said, "Well, if you're going to do it, it'll be without the kids and me."

I had suspected that that would be her answer, but when she said it, the words went through me like a knife. I said, "Listen to reason, Marge. I really want you and the kids with me. This is the biggest opportunity of my life. It's the time you *should* be here. We're gonna make it big now, honey."

She said, "You're out of your mind, doing this crazy thing. You know, you're nuts. I want out of this maniac plot."

I knew she meant it and I pleaded with her to reconsider, but it was too late. It had been over for a long time, but this was the last straw.

I didn't know where to go. I felt alone and dejected; so I called my dad. I hadn't seen too much of him in the past few months because I had been so busy. I had helped him with the down payment on his house a couple of years before—it had only been a couple of hundred dollars, but I had been saving it for a super-charger and he had said half of the house was mine. "Dad," I said, "I'm getting a divorce because of this jet car and I don't have anyplace to go. Can I come and live with you?"

He said, "Come on, Craig. You're always welcome here."

My dad was a special effects man at Sam Goldwyn Studios and my situation sounded to him like the plot from one of the science fiction movies he was working on. Here I was, involved with a 40-foot monster and my wife was walking out on me because I loved it more than I did her. I think he said yes because it would probably be good for his career to live with a real-life science fiction star.

The plot thickened. Goodyear's engineer called and said, "I know we told you we would supply tires, but there's this austerity program and we are just not going to be able to do it. We're sorry, kid, but we can't do it right now. We're cutting way back on our racing budget." That was that. Strike two.

By the time I got to the garage I was pretty upset. Ed Perkins was there waiting for me. It was unbelievable, but he put his arm around me and said, "Craig, I know I told you I would give you the $10,000 you need to get the car started, but business has been bad and I can't do it. You can keep the engine and you know you have my best wishes. I just can't put any more money in the car, son."

That was about it. I figured that racing, like baseball, was a three strike business, and I had had all three of them. The only trouble is that I felt that I had gone down with the bat on my shoulder. There hadn't even been anything I could swing at.

It was July 31, 1960. I had quit my job, my wife was divorcing me, I had lost my tire sponsor and my $10,000 — *and* the place to build the car, too. I was sitting here with a jet engine and nothing to do with it.

I went to my dad. I told him that my luck was down again and he could help me. All I wanted to do was knock the back out of the garage, extend it 20 feet, pour a concrete slab for a new addition, chop down the cherry tree (I didn't have the heart to say anything funny about George Washington), take down the badminton court and the barbecue grill, and move the back fence. I told him I would pay for the materials, do the work myself, and would build a better fence. As an added inducement, I told him he could fire the gardener, and I would take care of the lawn.

He muttered something about nobody believing it if they saw it in one of his movies and said, "Okay, go ahead."

I had enough friends around so that I could get the

supplies on credit and, as always, my buddies came to my aid and helped me with the backyard project. It was a three-ring circus, but everything was done in six weeks. We had a 40-foot-long garage and a new redwood fence, and I had even built a little shed out back to keep the gardening tools in. I never got around to using them, but at least they were in out of the rain and weeds.

I was living on unemployment compensation at the time. That's a story in itself. The only way I could get payment fast enough was to come up with a good reason for quitting my job — otherwise the procedure would take an eternity. So I told the unemployment bureau that I had quit my job at the fire department because I had had to drive the fire truck and the rescue truck and it scared me. I got my payments.

My next break occurred when two friends, Jim and Lucy Johnson, dropped by to see me one day. They offered to lend me the $10,000 I needed. Lucy was very wealthy, but I couldn't just take the money. "Tell you what I'll do," I said. "I have this lot in Palm Springs that I managed to save from the divorce settlement and it's worth ten grand. I'll sell it to you." They agreed and I was back in business.

They gave me $3,500 and said they would give me the rest later. They couldn't let me have it all at once; it had something to do with taxes. But the $3,500 would at least get me out of debt, help me with my child-support payments, and get me back to work on the jet car.

Whatever the tax problem was, it had completely tied up their money, and things started to get tough for me again almost at once. The first $3,500 was gone, and it seemed that everything was turning sour again. I had started building the car, the garage was full of junk, the money was running out—and, at that point, my dad flipped and said it would be better if I just got out of the house. He couldn't take it anymore. The studio had started to seem more like real life than his life at home.

The frame of the car was partially built and the engine was in it. Things had really started taking shape. What could I do now? You just don't move into an apartment with a 40-foot-long monstrosity behind you and say, "Oh, by the way, this comes, too."

During the six months that the garage-building and jet car program had been driving my dad to distraction, I had been dating Lee Roberts, a car-hop at a drive-in just down the street from the house. Lee was divorced and had two kids of her own; so we had a lot in common. I guess we both felt pretty lonely and bitter about marriage at first, when we started going out after she got off work. I had been working extra hard to help take my own problems off my mind, and the diversion helped a lot. On days when my children were allowed to visit me, we took them *and* Lee's two to the beach.

So, when my dad asked me to move, Lee was the first person I thought of. My mom and step-dad had moved all the way out to Malibu to get away from the city, and I needed somebody to turn to. I went over to the drive-in and waited for Lee to get off work. We drove out to Manhattan Beach to watch the surf, and I told her that I had this run-in with my dad and that he had thrown me out. She said that her uncle, with whom she and her kids lived, had an extra room and that she was sure he would rent it to me and wouldn't be too upset if he didn't get his rent right away. Lee knew how desperate my money situation was and probably went home and told her uncle that *she* would pay my rent if I couldn't. At any rate, I took the room and continued to work on the car in the garage back of dad's house—that was part of the deal with him when I left. I saw Lee a lot more often after that.

My dad got married shortly afterward and his wife had a fit over my working on the car, even if I was *outside* the house. There was a lot of noise, with weird people running around all of the time; so I really couldn't blame her. We talked it over and I asked my dad if he would trade me his half of the house for the lot I "had" in Palm Springs, which he could sell for $10,000. Dad said it sounded like a good deal. Then I went to Jim and Lucy and said, "Look, you were going to buy my lot for $10,000 but so far you've only paid me $3,500 and you can't pay me any more. I'm broke, my dad threw me out, and he's going to sell the house. I don't have anyplace and Lee is in this apartment, and . . . "

At this point I was starting to turn blue from the long list of tragedies that had befallen me; so I was glad when Jim said, "Wait, Craig, I know. And we're sorry, but it's this tax thing."

I knew that Jim really had the hots for my coupe; so I said, "What I was going to ask is, would you take the coupe for the $3,500 and give me back the lot for my father, so I'll have a place to build this race car?"

Jim and Lucy said yes and gave me the lot.

It was like giving them my right arm when I handed them the keys to the coupe. I'd had it since I was 13, but it was all I had left. I felt like John Wayne giving away his horse. Boy, would I have made a crumby cowboy.

I moved into Lee's uncle's house, and shortly afterward Lee and I got married. It became quite a life. We had air ducts in the living room, and the whole place had been turned into a shop. There were jet engine parts all over the backyard and all types of steel tubing and frames in the driveway. The neighbors were going out of their trees — especially the ones who lived in the apartment house next door. They complained to the landlord, who was a man named Mr. Tuchen. One day Mr. Tuchen came down to talk to me and saw the horrible maze of stuff, with guys going in and out in trucks. It was terrible.

"What's this? What's this? What are you doing? What's this?" he asked.

I said, "This is my hobby, Mr. Tuchen. I'm a hot-rodder, and this is my hobby."

He almost came apart at this. "This is no hobby; it's a business," he screamed.

7. The Case of the Gorgeous Model

The jet car program was getting to the stage where I needed wind tunnel tests to prove the aerodynamic qualities of the design. The only practical and logical time to run the tests was, naturally, before the car was built, and it would have to be done with a specially-designed model. After the tests, we could easily make the necessary modifications to the design and, when the design was perfected, we could build the car exactly like the model.

Certainly the most important consideration in building any race car, particularly one in which you expect to go over 400 miles an hour, is its aerodynamic design — the main factor that makes a jet car different from an airplane. If it's designed improperly and doesn't have the necessary amount of negative lift, the car will fly. That wasn't exactly what we had in mind for going fast. The fact that this had happened to a number of land speed record attempt cars at the Salt Flats was constantly on my mind. Aerodynamics also plays another highly important role in the design of a race car. Proper aerodynamic design allows a car to go fast. *That* we did have in mind.

Art Russell and I had talked about a wind tunnel model while we were building the first one; so he wasn't at all surprised when I showed up at his house one evening with the first model and a stack of drawings. "What took you so long?" he asked.

However, to help guide us in making the model, we decided that before we started we should talk with someone who had wind tunnel knowledge. So it was back to the air guard, and once again they came through. Mike Freebairn contacted a fellow named Rod Schapel, who worked for Task Corporation. Rod had all of the qualifications. He was an aerodynamic engineer with vast experience in wind tunnel testing *and* a former racing enthusiast.

Rod was really interested in the model. He must have been because when I told him I didn't have any money to pay for the tests, he didn't throw me out of his office. He said that Task certainly couldn't test the car for nothing, but there might still be a way. He told us that if we built our own model the fellows at the Naval Post-graduate School in Monterey might do the testing for pretty close to nothing. They had been known to do a little moonlighting on weekends, and for a few dollars an hour he thought they might be persuaded to run a test on the model.

Rod made some suggestions and changes in my plans, and furnished Art and me with a new set of drawings with which to build the second model. We spent a lot of time on this one. It had three different nose configurations and two different sets of rear fenders that were removable. This way we could run it with or without the fenders — to determine the air drag of the exposed wheels — or with any of the three different noses. We had started to get pretty sophisticated.

Bill Moore, meanwhile, was working on more art work for a flip chart presentation that I hoped would get me some sponsors. Someplace along the line it would be nice if we came up with some money. I had sold about everything I owned and had taken a part-time job at a garage in Santa Monica just to get the money I needed for the fellows to do the wind tunnel testing. Lee was still working at the drive-in, but it took most of her salary just to feed us — us and the gang of people who were in and out constantly. It was like running a sandwich shop — there were a lot of people helping.

We spent three weekends in Monterey and came away with outstanding data on the aerodynamics of the car. We even had photographs, and *everything* looked encouraging. The tunnel test had proved the three-wheel configuration was the perfect design for the speeds we had in mind. I was ecstatic — broke, but ecstatic.

The next step was to name the car. We couldn't just keep calling it "jet car" or "it." The program was beginning to take shape and a name was important. Finding one didn't take long. I had always been patriotic, and I wanted a name that was worthy of the car that would bring the world's land speed record back to the United States. I had built a model of Charles Lindberg's plane, "The Spirit of St. Louis," when I was a kid and for some unknown reason this popped right into my head. Then it hit me — the perfect combination of patriotism and adventure — *The Spirit of America!*

The name probably didn't impress Mr. Tuchen as much as it did me, because things at the house were getting more and more hectic by the moment. Here was the plot: Walt Sheehan had finalized the drawings of the air inlets. I had contacted a pattern maker by the name of Frank Fellows, to help me with building the molds for these huge inlet ducts. Walt and Frank were coming over every night, along with another friend, Henry Brown, who worked for H. I. Thompson Fiber Glass. Henry was invaluable with the fiber glass engineering and lay up. This was a complicated process that entailed laying weaves of cloth in with the fiber glass. It had to be done properly or the ducts would not have the necessary strength.

Ted Thal of Thalco, one of the foremost fiber glass industry pioneers, had given me the glass and resin — components used in our fiber glass construction.

This frantic activity was going on in the living room. The plaster cores that Frank and I had made (around which the fiber glass ducts were to be formed) were about ten feet long and were works of art. They were hand-finished and lacquered to the configuration of the inside of the ducts. The procedure used in building them was complicated. After they were built, it was necessary to putty, sand, block, and lacquer them — they had to be just perfect. Then we had to lay fiber glass over the molds. When they were all done, we had huge ducts that weighed about 300 pounds each.

We had sprayed a parting agent over them before we laid the fiber glass, but after we broke the cores out, there were still tiny chunks of plaster that stuck inside the ducts. This is where Lee came in. She was the only one small enough to crawl into the ducts and chip the little pieces out; so we would dress her in flannel pajamas and slide her down into the ducts with a hammer, chisel, and flashlight. She would stay in there for hours and was perfectly content with her chore — except when someone left the screen door open and our dachshund, Spirit, got in. The first time it happened, we heard Lee screaming and rushed in to find her stuck half in and half out of the mold, with Spirit sitting there licking the bottoms of her feet. After that it was a pretty routine thing. Lee would scream and one of us would matter-of-factly go in, pick up the dog, and put him out. He finally quit doing it because there was so much noise and activity outside that he was afraid to run the risk of being put out.

The whole inlet duct operation was very important. The ducts had to be perfect, their insides as smooth as glass. Building ducts that won't collapse for a jet engine is difficult because of the tremendous pressure that builds up as the jet engine gulps fantastic quantities of air. Dr. Ostich had run only once on the Flats with his jet car and had failed to do well because the ducts collapsed at only 60 percent power. Even the aircraft industry had its problems from time to time with this situation. They would get a plane completely designed, build a mock-up, and find that the inlet ducts just wouldn't stand the stress. In addition to this, no one, including the aircraft industry, had ever built a set of *fiber glass* ducts; so this was somewhat of a pioneering effort.

Anyway, we had the special weaves of cloth, all going in certain directions—twice as thick in the corners—and all feathered out. Man, it was intricate. The engineering and construction had to be perfect. Fortunately I had a design engineer, an experienced pattern maker, and a fiber glass expert to help me—not to mention Lee and Spirit.

All of this stuff and all of these people were arriving constantly. It was amazing. Bill and Art were working on the model in the dining room, which was also the drafting room. They were painting it and lettering the name on it. Everything was going together somehow with nothing—piece by piece and part by part. But it was going together amidst the most awful confusion I had ever seen.

On the day another truck load of supplies (this time it was some free tubing from a friend at the Tube Distributors in Los Angeles) and Mr. Tuchen arrived simultaneously—as a matter of fact, the truck almost ran over him—I realized the project had gotten out of hand. There were parts all over the backyard, air inlet ducts in the living room, a half-built trailer in the drive-way—a 40-foot Fruehauf van that I had borrowed from Ed—and a garage crammed full of material. Well, it was incredible. It was definitely out of hand, and if we didn't get a sponsor soon, the whole project would be down the drain—it would take not only me with it, but also a lot of my friends who had worked hard on the *Spirit*.

Art, Bill, and I quit everything else we were doing and put the finishing touches on the presentation. From that point on, it was Operation: Sponsor. It had to be. There was no money left and no more friends to give us supplies.

When we finished, the presentation was impressive. The flip chart was a masterpiece because Bill had done many for Hughes Aircraft and he knew what he was doing. And the model—it was gorgeous! We built a beautiful case for it, which made it look even more impressive. It was February 1, 1961, and I was ready.

Andy Anderson's Shell Station, on the corner of Se-pulveda and Venice boulevards, was an old hangout of mine. It was right across the street from the Clock Drive-in of my high school days. It was also the same corner where I used to wait for the people to pick me up to go to art class; so, one way or another, I had hung around there for years, and Andy and I had become good friends.

I had bought a '39 Ford pick-up for $150 and had painted it silver-frost blue. It had mahogany sideboards and was beautifully lettered "Craig Breedlove, Spirit of America, World's Land Speed Record Attempt." My business cards said the same thing. Now that I look back at it, that truck was pretty neat, and I had done a lot of restoring on it while waiting for one thing or another for the *Spirit*. It had rolled and tucked upholstery and a dark blue metallic grill and a fairly strong engine—the whole bit.

My attire wasn't quite as splendid because I didn't even own a suit. When I left home, I had three pairs of levis, a whole bunch of T-shirts with writing all over them, and one, that's right, one, sport shirt. So, I put on one of the clean pairs of levis and the sport shirt and polished up a pair of shoes that I had gotten for high school graduation. In fact, I only had one decent pair. The rest had been ruined in the garage.

Andy came out to talk with me as I parked the truck at the back of the station. "Who's in charge of the Shell district office next door, Andy?" I asked him. He told me a man named Bill Lawler was the district manager. I wrote the name down on one of my cards.

The receptionist at the Shell office looked a little surprised when I struggled through the door with the model case and flip charts. I told her my name was Breedlove and handed her my card. "I want to see Mr. Lawler, please," I said. With no appointment or anything, there I stood in all my splendor.

She opened the door to his office and said, "Mr. Lawler, there's a Mr. Breedlove to see you," and I heard this big, deep voice say, "Send him right in." The place shook a little bit and I thought, "Oh, boy, fasten your seat belt."

I trotted through the door with my "dog and pony show." He looked up in amazement and said, "You're not Victor Breedlove." I later learned that Mr. Lawler had a Shell dealer named Victor Breedlove, whom he had been expecting.

I took a deep breath and blurted out—in one sentence, I think—"No, sir, Mr. Lawler, I'm *Craig* Breedlove and I'm here to talk to you about a project that, I think, will not only benefit myself but Shell Oil Company as well, and I'm sure it will interest you because I am going to bring the world's land speed record back to the United States after an absence of 34 years, and after many people have tried and failed, and I have the car that can do it."

He looked up in bewilderment, took off his glasses, and said, "You've got ten minutes."

The flip chart presentation ran as smooth as silk. I had it down pat, and it was soon apparent to him that it was not only feasible, this wild and woolly scheme of mine, but it was a public relations gem. After an hour of charts and photos and wind tunnel test results, Mr. Lawler was on the edge of his chair.

The box with the model was in clear sight, but I hadn't said a word about it at this stage. Mr. Lawler kept looking at it and finally, when I paused at the end of the presentation, he could stand it no longer. "All right, what's in the box?" he bellowed.

I reached down and opened the mysterious box and all you could see was velvet lining and a piece of purple velvet covering an object. "Mr. Lawler," I said as I whisked the cloth off the gorgeous, *absolutely beautiful* model, "this is the *Spirit of America*."

Well, he just came straight up out of his chair and grabbed the thing out of my hands and disappeared through the door. I thought he had flipped. I could hear him running down the hall shouting, "Look at this! Look at this!"

Finally he came back and panted, "How long has it been since you've had a decent meal?"

I was truthful when I answered, "Quite a while."

"Well," he said, "I'm taking you to lunch."

At lunch he asked me if I really thought I was going to break the world's land speed record. "I don't think I'm going to break the record, Mr. Lawler; I *know* I'm going to break it," I answered him. We both knew I meant it.

He looked at me square in the eyes and said, "Craig, I know you are, too, and I'm going to do everything within my power to see that Shell Oil Company helps you do it."

Shell, like many giant corporations, is a conservative company, and the fact that I had sold a district manager on the project didn't mean that the company was *sold*. I had one tremendous advantage, however. Bill Lawler was a persistent man, and this project became almost as important to him as it did to me—and he was a super-salesman. As a matter of fact, he is now a vice-president of Shell; so he was no ordinary district manager.

The next step, Bill Lawler said, was to muster enough force on the West Coast to interest the big wigs back in New York; otherwise they wouldn't even bother coming out to talk about it. "Do you have a suit?" he asked. I told him I didn't but that I would get one somehow if he thought I needed one.

"Well, you need one, and you need it Monday. That's the day we're going to sell Al Hines," he said. Al Hines was a division manager and a close personal friend of Sid Golden, Shell's vice-president in charge of marketing.

I went down to Jim Clinton Clothes and for $35 bought a suit, tie, and dress shirt. It was high school graduation all over again, except this time I hoped I was graduating from the ranks of the starving.

Well, we sold Al Hines and then a vice-president from San Francisco. It was all part of Bill's strategy to entice Sid Golden to the West Coast to see the plans. The three of them wrote to him, but he said flatly, "No, we're not sponsoring some crazy kid and his wingless airplane and that's it."

That answer would have been enough for most people, but not Bill Lawler. He wrote right back and said, "Listen, you can't turn this thing down without even seeing it."

I guess his persistence got through because Sid Golden wrote back and told him that he was going to be on the Coast the next week to see his son off to the Marine Corps and he would talk to them about it.

When Golden arrived, Bill and Al met him at the bar of his hotel. They let him get about three martinis under his belt before they really started to work on him. "All right, all right, I'll look at this jet or whatever it is."

The meeting was set for the next afternoon. I spent most of the night working on the presentation and perfecting the unveiling of the model. When I arrived at the Shell office, Bill came out and said, "I hope you've got your selling cap on, kid, because this guy's tough. Besides, there were a lot of martinis last night and, well, he's not feeling too good." I almost dropped the model case.

The presentation went even better than it had the first time. At the very end I proudly thrust the model in his hands and said, "Mr. Golden, can you imagine one of these models in every home in the United States with a Shell emblem on it?"

He just looked at it and said, "Yes, I can. You've got something. I'm going to okay this project on one condition—that our engineering group investigate it and give us a positive okay that it's sound in engineering and design, and we're not getting into anything that someone's going to get killed in."

I knew I had made it because I knew that the car *was* sound in every aspect. I was especially gentle with the model as I put it back into the case because I knew that a new age of racing had been born and this was its first child.

As soon as the Shell engineers approved the project, I went straight to the telephone. I knew Shell's decision would give me leverage with Goodyear. I called Walt Devinney, the racing tire engineer who had been to see me earlier, and said, "Walt, I have Shell Oil Company as a sponsor for the jet car. Can you see if the picture has changed any there?"

Devinney was a little stunned, but he finally said, "You really have Shell? You mean Shell Oil in New York?"

"That's the one," I told him.

"Let me do some checking, Craig, and I'll call you right back," he said.

Shell was about a $30-million-a-year customer of Goodyear. Bill Lawler had told me that certainly Goodyear would now be a lot more willing to consider my project.

Walt called back and said, "Can you come to Akron, Craig, to talk with some of our people?"

I was on a plane next morning, and when I got there I learned that the "some of our people" were Russell DeYoung, president; Vic Holt, executive vice-president; Mike Miles, vice-president in charge of sales; Bob Lane, director of public relations; Tony Webner, director of racing; and Walt Devinney. It was quite an impressive group for a 23-year-old hot-rodder, but I had the presentation polished to a fine hue, and I had Shell behind me. There would be no more of this David and Goliath action for me—I already had one giant under my belt.

Well, when I got in that board room and looked at

the long table and the important-looking surroundings and the important-looking people, I was shakier than David had ever been. I prayed that my slingshot would hold out.

After the presentation, Vic Holt said, "Craig, I guess what you want to know now is whether Goodyear will build tires and help you financially, is that right?"

"That's right, Mr. Holt. I'm very interested in that," I said meekly.

Holt asked Walt to take me down and show me around some of the tire-making operations while they discussed the matter. We left the room, took an elevator down to the main floor, and walked back into the plant. I didn't have too much to say because, well, I guess, because my heart was in my mouth. Fortunately, we didn't have too long to wait. Walt got a phone call in the plant, and when he came back, he looked at me and said, "You've got it, Craig. They said yes."

I leaned against a pillar and the realization hit me—the realization of what I had put together. It *all* had to be ready by summer. Mr. Tuchen was right. It really wasn't a hobby; now it *was* a business.

8.

Good-bye, Mr. Tuchen

Quinn Epperly did what the breakfast cereal commercials talk about—he built strong bodies. However, he built them for race cars, and they were not only strong—they were beautifully done. Now I had money and *he* was a natural choice to build the body for the *Spirit of America.*

Quinn came over to the garage and just stood there in disbelief when he saw this 40-foot-long frame sitting amidst the debris from six months of hectic efforts. He was accustomed to building bodies for Indianapolis cars, which were about one-third the size of the *Spirit,* and the whole thing was a little overwhelming. He just stood there, shaking his head and saying, "It's the biggest thing I've ever seen."

He stepped back about ten feet, took another long look and said, "Bring it over to the shop."

The next day Goodyear sent over four truck wheels and tires, so that we could shift the car around while they were designing and building the rear wheels and tires. Now we could move it—move it, that is, if it weren't for a few minor problems. The car was eleven and one-half feet wide, and I had to get it out of the garage and down the driveway. It was like building a boat in the basement. There were some obstacles, namely, the fence, the side porch, and Mr. Tuchen's hedge. They all had to go.

77

I didn't want to take a chance on Mr. Tuchen's saying no when it came to cutting down the hedge; so I thought we had better get to it early in the morning before he got up. I had always known my early hedge-trimming days would come in handy. This, however, was to be my swan song.

Mr. Tuchen would probably be so relieved to see the car go that the loss of his hedge would be insignificant, I reasoned. At least I felt that I could convince him of it because I had had a lot of experience in calming Mr. Tuchen down after every crisis. But he did have a for sale sign in the front of his apartment building. We had just about driven him out; so the car's leaving might be his most glorious moment.

We got up early, and the first thing we did was to cut down the hedge. Then we tore out the fence, broke up the steps, and started to move the *Spirit* down the driveway. Officials from Shell and Goodyear were there and all of the neighbors and hundreds of passers-by. It was a real traffic jam. And right in the middle of it stood Mr. Tuchen, with a smile on his face like the Mona Lisa. He hadn't even noticed that his hedge was gone. I walked over to him and said, "It's about the hedge, Mr. Tuchen. We'll plant a new one tommorow. We'll plant a whole new hedge." He looked at me with this funny smile and far off look in his eyes — the look of a man completely at peace with the world.

"A new hedge. A new hedge. Okay, okay," he said.

The house was all but demolished by the time we moved the car and all of the people over to Quinn's shop. It's a good thing that we moved, for the car was no longer the project of a bunch of *buddies* — they had now been replaced by a lot of *employees*. I realized that I had to learn a lot, with half a dozen guys on the payroll and an honest to goodness deadline to meet.

Before, it had been pretty much my own schedule, and I could go at any pace I pleased. I couldn't set the schedule anymore. It was May and the car had to be completed by August. August was when conditions at the Salt Flats were best, and Shell and Goodyear had planned a press conference for August 9. We had to be ready by August.

It took a lot of organizing because Quinn also had six guys working on the project. This meant that we had to keep 12 people busy at all times *and* the work rolling in the proper direction.

Goodyear was also working against a deadline because they had just started to design the tires and wheels, and they had to be built and tested extensively. I talked with them a lot, and they had people coming around all the time to look at my wind tunnel data and talk with me about the salt and other factors. I felt pretty flattered that a company the size of Goodyear would place that much confidence in my judgment. It made me work even harder.

It had taken *two years* to get the car to that point; it had to be completely finished in *three months*. The tremendous strain changed my personality somewhat. I was no longer the jovial kid down the street with a hot rod and trophies and a lot of fantastic dreams. I was a businessman and a foreman on a big project sponsored by two giant companies, and I became all business—not to the point of being unfair and hateful to the guys, it's true, but I was firm. Before, I had been easygoing and trusting with everybody. With the business I was now running, I didn't have time for any of that. The car couldn't have been further from a hobby.

Fortunately, the fellows understood the deadline problems, and we worked 18 or 20 hours a day on the car. We didn't stop, and some of the guys would work until they dropped. Then they would sleep on the floor. It was a complete, out-and-out crash program. It also wasn't long until the payroll became a crash program, too.

I had told Shell that I thought it would take $30,000 to complete the car, but we went through most of that in the first month. So, for the second time in 30 days, I was back in Bill Lawler's office with my hands out. I told him that the whole thing was costing much more than I had ever anticipated, and he listened attentively.

"The body's costing three times as much as I expected, and the guys are working around the clock," I said. "Before everybody was working for nothing, and the thirty thousand sounded like all the money in the world. Now it's a business, and we're paying everybody a salary. Nobody's *giving* us anything anymore, and we're just spending money like it's going out of style."

He let me finish and then he said, "I've got some good news for you. We knew you couldn't do it for $30,000; so we appropriated $75,000." Shell must have marked it up to "education" — *my* education. I just hadn't realized that it was going to cost so much, what with buying everything and paying everybody.

The next problem that we faced was the design of the car's steering. Because of the car's triangular shape, it was difficult to design front wheel steering, and Rod Schapel, who had agreed to help me with the final design, had wrestled with the problem for a month. Finally he decided that we should steer the car by using differential braking on the back. In other words, we would steer it the way you steer some old tail-dragger airplane. You step on the right brake and it makes a retarding movement on that side of the car, causing it to veer in that direction.

The plan was that I was going to steer the car with the brakes until I got up to 150 miles an hour. At that point I would have sufficient air speed to be able to guide the car with the fin that would be placed on the bottom of the nose. It would be just like taxiing it up to air speed and then steering with the fin, as if we were going to fly an airplane.

The idea didn't appeal to me at first because I couldn't imagine a car that didn't steer entirely with a steering wheel, but the more Rod talked to me about it, the more convinced I was that it would work. That's the way the car was built.

Spirit of America was completed on schedule—August 9, 1961, exactly on the day of the press conference. If I'd had any idea of just what Shell and Goodyear had in mind, I'm not sure that I would have made it. I would have had stage fright. The unveiling was held at the Beverly Hills Country Club, and we looked like the original Beverly Hillbillies by the time we arrived. We worked on the car—polishing and buffing and touching it up, right up to the gate of the country club—and it was fantastically beautiful, even if we weren't. As soon as the car was positioned near the eighteenth green in this spectacular sylvan setting, we ducked out the back and got cleaned up in the locker room.

When the press (and it seemed as if there were a thousand reporters) arrived, there was a magnificent blue and silver three-wheeled car with about the sleekest lines of anything in the world. The workmanship was superb, and it glistened like $100,000—because that's what it had cost.

All the Shell and Goodyear VIP's were there, and even people like General Jimmy Dolittle. The unveiling was a tremendous success. I talked to all of the wire services and television networks and racing writers, and for the first time I really knew that there was something *more* to this whole thing than just a hot-rodding kid's dream. This really was the "spirit of America."

After the press conference we all took a couple of days off and just rested. We were totally exhausted, and most of us hadn't had a decent night's sleep in three months — just an hour or two here and there, whenever we could find time. Most of the fellows just went somewhere and collapsed.

My retreat was Redondo Beach, and Lee and I lay in the sun and played in the surf. We were like a couple of kids again. It was the first time in three years that I had taken off *one* day to do something for myself, and I was determined to enjoy every second of it. I hadn't gone to a restaurant — except for business purposes — or a movie or a dance in so long I couldn't remember. That first night Lee and I had dinner at a neat little seafood place at the beach and went to a movie afterward. I wore my new blue blazer with the Spirit of America emblem on the pocket.

When we got back to earth — which, in this case, was Quinn's shop — Rod and I sat down and started to finalize the program, so that everybody would know his job when we got to the Flats. This had to be done immediately because we had learned that conditions were perfect at the Salt Flats. We all knew that the situation could change with the first storm; so we had better get there, soon.

It was apparent that my time was going to be taken up with learning to drive the new car, and with the questions and interviews of the army of newsmen who were planning to be there. I wouldn't have much time to run the crew; so I asked Rod to take over that duty.

He would be the project manager. I would tell him how I thought the car was handling and what I thought needed adjusting and he would then work with Nye Frank, the chief mechanic, and between them, the work would get done.

We were ready to go, and fortunately for us, our competition had problems. Dr. Ostich had run his jet car but hadn't done too well because the inlet ducts again collapsed and the car had a shimmying problem. Mickey Thompson had all but given up temporarily but was talking of putting rockets on the *Challenger* to try to get it going faster. Donald Campbell had crashed the *Bluebird,* which was being rebuilt in England. Athol Graham crashed his *City of Salt Lake* and had been killed. Glenn Leasher was ready to come to the Flats in a jet-powered car built by Romeo Palamedes. The latter was an after-burning J-47 powered car that was essentially a four-wheeler with a Ford front axel under it. It was pretty much a hot rod with a jet engine.

That was what we were up against, and we were confident. We were ready and well organized, and our spirits were high.

Earl Heath has lived in Wendover, Utah, all his life, and he has seen the best of the LSR cars come and go. He owns the Western Motel and Cafe and the service station where most of the work is done on the race cars. He helps the state of Utah manage the Salt Flats. In two words he is the resident expert on all matters pertaining to land speed racing.

When he came out of his restaurant to see the *Spirit of America*, I knew that his pronouncement would be picked up by Salt Lake City newspapers and relayed to the world press. He took one look at the car, slapped his forehead, and said, "You just set the competition back 30 years." That kind of newspaper copy we could use.

We took all of the equipment out to the Flats and got the crew started setting up camp. It was a pretty big job: we had a 40-foot van loaded with tools and equipment, the car had to be wheeled off the flat-bed trailer it was on, and the generator truck had to be unloaded. I guess Earl was right. Most LSR attempts had been so much of a shoestring nature that this looked like Ringling Brothers and Barnum and Bailey had just rolled into town. When the crew got the striped tent set up, the townspeople would be convinced that it was a circus.

The trip was a little awesome to me, too. For one

thing, it was the first time I had ever stayed in a *motel* in Wendover. So far as I was concerned, Salt Flats racing was a sleep in the car or on the ground proposition — we could be close to the cars and the action that way, we had reasoned. Actually, it had been all we could afford in those less affluent days.

In 1961, however, we moved into the Wendover Motel, and I was staggered to learn that we actually occupied 21 rooms — engineers, public relations men, and the crew of the *Spirit*. I had a large, second-floor, double room on the end. I went in and plopped down in the chair beside the bed. What luxury! My sleeping on the Flats days had ended. I had never admitted it even to myself before, but it used to get pretty cold out there at night.

When I could tear myself away from the room, I decided to take a walk. A walk in Wendover is usually a fairly short affair because there really isn't much to the town. What there is, however, is picturesque and is completely out of place as a setting for land speed racing. The town looks as if it's just popped right out of every Western movie you've ever seen. I'm still convinced that most of them were filmed there, although Earl Heath claims they weren't. The feeling is there — particularly at the railroad station.

The station is a squat, one-story, frame building that had to be moved there from the Twentieth Century-Fox lot. I always expected the 5:20 to come rolling in with steam hissing out of wherever it is that steam hisses from. Ava Gardner would step down from one of the cars, and Spencer Tracy would amble out of the station and say, "Help you, ma'am?" "It's the Kelly place I'm looking for," she would purr. He'd answer, "If you'll wait right there, I'll hitch up the buckboard and take you out myself."

The rest of the town fit in pretty well. There were a lot of dirt streets and adobe houses, and the mountains and foothills came right down into the town. Main Street was a little different. The horseless carriages that boiled into town from the 110-mile drive across the Great Salt Lake Desert were in desperate need of service stations. And service stations there were along Main Street—Route 40. There were no sidewalks, just driveways into the gas stations. The motels and the gambling casino were down at the end of Main Street—just across the border in Wendover, Nevada. The State Line Casino was mecca, the only escape from boredom.

It was as if all of these things were unfolding for me for the first time. Before, I had seen nothing but race cars and hot-rodders.

By the time I stepped back through the looking glass, some of the crew had returned from the Salt Flats. They had encountered some problems with the engine, and Rod had decided that we should take the car over to the nearly abandoned Wendover Air Force Base and work on it there. The wind was blowing fairly hard on the Flats; so it would be a lot better to take the side panels off in a hangar. The walls would keep the salt from blowing into the bearings and other exposed parts while Rod and his crew were making the necessary adjustments.

Finally, we got the engine running perfectly and headed for the Salt Flats. It was late in the afternoon, August 18. I knew that we had to hurry to get the car off the trailer if I expected to make a run that day. However, things ran smoothly and the car was wheeled to the International Course, the smoothest stretch of salt that could be found on the great expanse of the flat, white saline basin.

The Flats are a geological freak of nature, duplicated in only a few other places throughout the world. The one in Utah, moreover, is larger than most and smoother, and therefore faster, than *any* other. It had taken eons of time for nature to produce the great salt bed. The spring runoff from the mountain changes the surface yearly. Each spring, in fact, state road crews from the state of Utah, which owns the Flats, select the best eleven miles for a course. The crews then take care of it throughout the season, which usually doesn't start until August, after the summer rains, and continues until September, as a rule. Sometimes the season is shorter if storms move in early; occasionally it is longer. Sometimes there is no season at all—the surface stays flooded all year from unusually heavy spring and summer downfalls.

Once the weather breaks and the course is selected, the United States Auto Club moves a timing shack and miles of wire onto the salt. The wire is necessary to set up the timing lights and radio equipment. USAC is the official timing body, and all LSR cars must use its services to certify the speeds for a world record.

The eleven-mile course is divided into three sections, a five-mile buildup, a measured mile where timing takes place and average speed is calculated, and a five-mile section for stopping the car. A single black line distinguishes the course from the rest of the similar-looking terrain. It is necessary to make a run through the measured mile in each direction for an official record. The average time of the two runs is calculated to determine the official speed.

USAC submits the time to either the Fédération Internationale Automobile or the Fédération Internationale Motocycliste for world record sanctioning. The former sanctions four-wheeled vehicles; the latter, those with fewer than four wheels. So, technically, the *Spirit* was a motorcycle, but that didn't bother me. All I wanted was to go faster than anybody else had ever gone. A 38-foot, 10,000-horsepower motorcycle would be fine, thank you.

Joe Petrali, chief timer for USAC, was at the starting line at the north end of the course, where the car sat. "The salt is good this year, Craig," he said. "There are a few rough spots in the buildup, but the measured mile is smooth and you should have no trouble with the south end of the course." I needed the assurance. Of course, I had driven over the track, but it needed an experienced eye to tell whether the course was good.

I thanked Joe and walked toward the *Spirit*. The car was so big that it took a step ladder for me to get into the cockpit. As I mounted the first few steps I thought to myself, "This is a far cry from your first trip here." I looked at the tail of the car, where the jet blast would come out, and wondered for a fraction of a second what I was doing there. The wonder passed quickly and I eased into the seat, which had been molded to fit my body, and slipped the shoulder harness into place.

I looked around the car and then down to the ground. The instrument-laden panel stared back at me as I glanced around the cockpit. I looked at the horde of people standing around waiting for me to get the show on the road, and I thought, "So this is what the big league looks like."

I slipped my helmet on and buckled the strap. Nye, a crew member, who had come up the ladder, leaned into the cockpit and helped me fasten my breathing mask into place. In case of fire, the foam that would be automatically released, filling the cockpit, would make breathing impossible. I took a deep breath, and the cool compressed dry air filled my lungs. Everything had started to look unreal and mechanical.

The plan was to blast off at full power and zap right up to about 150 or 200, trying the two brake pedals to see if the steering was properly adjusted. Then, if all went well, I would back off the throttle and hold it at 200 MPH for a mile or two, and try the front fin to see if it was set right. If everything was still in order, I would make a run back, from north to south for the first leg of the record.

Nye slipped the canopy into place, and I fastened it from the inside with two large twist handles. The stepladder was moved away. The starting generator was in place, and I nodded to Nye. The high-pitched whine of the engine pierced the stillness of the Flats and I sat there. Now, it was just me and my car. I thought of all of the years I had spent getting there. It had all started with a bicycle; I had at last reached the three-wheeler stage.

I held the car with the brakes and advanced the hand throttle to 70 percent power. I took a deep breath of air, gave the okay sign, and took my feet off the brakes. The car started to move, and I shoved the throttle to 100 percent power.

I thought I had known what acceleration was before, but when I shoved that throttle forward, the force was astounding. I was glued to the seat and I had the sort of feeling in the pit of my stomach that you get in a car when you go over a big dip in the road at high speed. The only difference was that this feeling just stayed there, like I was going over the biggest dip in the world — maybe the Grand Canyon.

In a second or two I was over the initial sensation, and I realized that the car was veering off the track to the right. I stepped on the left brake; the car zoomed right back on the track and off the left side of the course. I hit the right brake, and the whole thing repeated itself. It was like a series of zigzags, back and forth. I tried the fin, and nothing happened. By then I was up to about 240 MPH and out of control. I was completely over my head and hanging onto the wheel for dear life: so I reached over and slammed the engine off.

I sat there and said to myself, "What is going on?" The car had absolutely gotten away from me. I hadn't had any control over it at all. I was totally bewildered and mad, and so completely disappointed that I could have cried.

Rod was one of the first to get to the car. "What's wrong? Why did you shut it off?" he asked.

I told him that nothing worked. "The brakes didn't work, the fin didn't work, nothing," I said. He didn't believe it.

"They had to work," he screamed.

"Well, I'm telling you right now they didn't," I answered. "I was out there still trying to steer it with the brakes at 240. The fin didn't work."

We quit for the day and went back to the motel. I sat there in my room and tried to go over everything that could have gone wrong. I finally decided that I was going to have to start from the very bottom and get used to the car. It would be better to start tomorrow by idling the car down the salt and then, little by little, up the power output until we found out what was causing the problems. I went over to see Rod, and he agreed.

This car had 10,000 horsepower—the average Indianapolis car has 500 and a hot passenger car 350—and I had started running it flat out. I couldn't tell what was happening, because of the tremendous force the acceleration had placed on everything. I did well, I felt, to hang on, let alone diagnose any problems.

So, the next morning I idled the car down the Flat at about 90 or 100 MPH, and when it started off to the right, I stepped on the left brake. It would start left, and then it might stop or arbitrarily decide to go right again. It was inconsistent despite the fact that the crew made every adjustment they could think of.

The hassle began to get out of hand, and Rod seemed to feel as if his golden chance as a designer was in jeopardy. He just sort of lost touch with finding the problem and spent more time trying to justify the design than trying to find out what was wrong.

We went through a solid week of this until the morale of the crew was completely shot. Rod was implying that I had lost my nerve and that this was the problem. The crew—and the sponsors—didn't know what to believe. I practically had a mutiny on my hands.

Then Nye discovered that a bearing that held the front wheel yoke in position was sliding back and forth in its housing, allowing the wheel to turn whatever way it wanted. The bearing was behaving like a swivel caster, and the wheel turned however it wanted to turn. The problem had been difficult to diagnose only because the condition didn't exist when the car was at rest, with all of the weight on the front wheel.

The discovery of the fault came all but too late. The whole thing had turned into a nightmare, and I had almost lost control of the situation. The whole organization was a shambles. Even finding the problem didn't help much, because the crew no longer wanted to do anything.

Never before had I been in a situation in which everybody was upset. I didn't know whether they were uptight with me or the car or what, but I did think that they were all calling me "chicken" behind my back. That was about to drive me nuts. I had dreamed of this opportunity all of my life, and now I was about to lose

it. I knew that I had to get over my persecution complex somehow, or it was all over. Somehow I mustered
up the necessary courage, smiled, and got back in the
car. I knew it was hopeless, but I wasn't going to give
in. I wasn't going to go down with the bat on my
shoulder this time.

I made a few more runs after correcting the problem,
but the fin still wouldn't steer the car. It *was* hopeless.
At this point, Rod called me a liar and said that I was
steering the car off the course on purpose, just to make
him and his design look bad.

I told him, "The car doesn't take an ignition key; so
get in and drive it yourself."

He said, "I would, but I can't fit in it." That was the
first point at which we had agreed in two weeks.

In the meantime Glenn Leasher had arrived and was
warming up in the bullpen. Yet, there I was with a
$100,000 car and two of the largest corporations in the
world behind me, and I couldn't make it. The *Spirit*
had plenty of power, it was clean, and the drag factor
was low enough for the car to break the record, but I
couldn't steer it. All I could envision was Leasher moving in with this hot rod with an old Ford axle under it
and, just because his front wheels would steer the car,
clipping off the record.

On the other hand, I could see only disaster if *we*
continued. If we stayed on while Leasher was there,
the press would make us look like a bunch of donkeys;
so I went to Bill Lawler of Shell and told him I wanted
to take the car home and put steering in it.

I said, "You can listen to Rod if you want to, but I've
spent three years of my life working on this car for one
purpose—to break the land speed record. I won't stay
up here and see Shell and Goodyear made fools of by a
car built in some guy's backyard—just because he can

steer it. I want to go home and fix the steering right, and come back. Otherwise I'm stepping out of it."

As usual, Bill heard me out. When I had finished, he stared out across the Salt Flats and said, "Okay, that's it. We're going home."

Just as we were ready to put the car on the trailer, one of the guys looked at the linkage that went to the front fin and found out that it had somehow been put into an adjustment that allowed it to move only about half an inch, lock to lock. The fin had been immobile during the whole time and no one had checked it. It was that simple: *no one had looked at it.* The whole program had been blown when I allowed someone else to step in and take over *my* project. That simple fact burned deep impressions into my mind, and I vowed that it would never happen again.

We made one more run with the fin in a high ratio, and I found that I could get some steering but it was marginal. Certainly, there was insufficient improvement to continue the run. The whole operation had to be demolished. We loaded up the car and started for home.

We were on the San Bernadino Freeway just outside of Los Angeles when we heard the news on the truck radio. Glenn Leasher had crashed and was dead. Suddenly the whole jet car program seemed to be insanity. I slumped over the wheel with tears in my eyes.

The First Four Hundred

The torture I went through after I got back to Los Angeles was extreme. Shell decided to bring in an impartial committee of engineers to study the project and advise them what to do; so I had to sit through countless hours of engineering meetings, going over the same points time and time again. The decision was really whether Shell was going to accept my recommendations for a steerable front wheel and vertical stabilizer or just abandon the whole sticky mess.

The strain was so great on me that I couldn't even eat properly. Often when I tried, I got severe pains in my chest. I felt emotionally lacerated—the meetings went on for five months! I had never faced this kind of a situation before. When I was planning and building the car, it had been all my show. *I* had decided what should be done, and I had the final say on *every* issue—large or small. In Los Angeles all I could do was sit in the meetings and *answer* when I was asked a question; I couldn't even relieve my frustrations by working harder, as I had done in the past, because there was nothing to work *on.*

The engineers finally arrived at the decision: the car would have steering and a tail fin! It was as if someone had taken 4,000 pounds off my back.

First, however, before we made any modifications to the car, I got some movie film of the Leasher crash from a Salt Lake City television station and studied it. I wanted to know what had caused the car to crash so that we could avoid the same mistake. I didn't learn much, but the film probably did more to reunite the crew than any other thing. It made them realize that driving a big jet car, even at 240 MPH as I had done, was not the same as driving down the freeway. We became a tightly knit group again.

Then another thing happened to make the sponsors feel that all of the decisions on the program had been right. Continental Casualty Company returned half of the insurance premium money because of our decision to stop running the car when it wasn't functioning exactly right.

At last everybody was solidly behind me again. I felt completely relaxed for the first time in six months.

The first modification task was to design an intricate steering system: a movable front wheel that operated in conjunction with the nose fin. The Goodyear engineers said it would work; so we installed the system and added an eight-foot tail fin to the car. After the fin had been spray-painted to match the car, a large American flag was painted on each side.

We decided we would like to test the car at the Los Angeles International Airport, but we had some difficulty getting permission. We called airline after airline and asked if we could use their taxiways, but they all said, flatly, No. Finally, and with mounting desperation, we made our last call, to Continental Airlines, and it was with great relief that we heard them say, "Sure, bring it over. We've been hearing a lot about the car, and our people would love to see it."

Continental and Shell arranged for airport permission to use the taxiway. It was a wild sight to see the big jets being routed around us. I can imagine what it looked like to the passengers in the taxiing airplanes, who probably thought some plane had come in for a landing and had ripped off its wings. I doubt that the sight did much for their morale.

A large crowd had gathered by the time we were ready to run, and only then did it strike me how paradoxical the situation was. Here were all these people watching breathlessly for a car to run about 200 MPH, yet when I got to the Salt Flats to break the world's land speed record, to run at about 400 MPH, there would be nobody there but the crew and the press. The difference, of course, was that we were in highly populated Los Angeles while for the record run, we would be on the moon — or someplace almost as remote.

The airport run was as routine as testing a new car off a showroom floor. I put my gear on, got in, fastened the canopy, and zapped down the runway at 200 *MPH*. The steering worked beautifully, and I found I could control the car perfectly. All we had to do was load it up and invite everybody to the Flats to watch the breaking of the world's land speed record.

I told the crew we would leave at five the next morning and they smiled in unison.

"Let's go home and get some rest, Champ," Nye said to me.

"Yeah, I guess we'll need it," I answered.

That night I thought a lot about the record and what it would mean to me. This "Spirit of America" thing had gotten to me, and I was proud of the concept. Stan Goldstein and I and some of the other guys on the crew I had gone to school with had voted in our first presidential election in 1960, and we were proud to be Americans. In fact, I think President Kennedy's inaugural speech — the part where he said, "Ask not what your country can do for you, but rather what you can do for your country" — impressed us more than anything else. I was young and I felt that I just had to do *something*. I couldn't very well win a Nobel prize—I wasn't equipped for anything like that—so I was going to do what I *was* equipped for: bringing the world's land speed record back to the United States.

Next morning we were on our way, a new and revitalized organization. I had gotten some pretty deep scars from the year before, and in August, 1963, I was well aware of the tremendous importance of really communicating with the guys in the crew. I knew that I had to stay close to them and work *with* them to maintain a sense of rapport and to keep the thing going. Some of them were coming back for the second year, and we all knew that we were lucky to be getting a second chance at bat. It would be our last chance; this one had to be good.

Everything was all business. *I* was running the show, and I expected it to run like a well-oiled clock. Thus, when we arrived at the Flats shortly before noon on August 3, 1963, we went straight to work—we didn't even stop in Wendover. We unloaded the van, set the tent up, got the generator truck in position, and rolled the car off the trailer. Everything moved smoothly. Everybody had a job to do, and I made sure it was done. I had a job to do myself.

When we had wheeled the car into position, I tightened the stop on the hand throttle at 70 percent power. We had installed a throttle regulator so that I wouldn't have to take my eyes off the track while I was at speed or to worry about giving the car too much power. The 70 percent setting should give us about 275 to 300 MPH, and I planned to make a few runs at that speed until I got used to the steering and the handling of the car.

On the first run I roared down the salt at 290 MPH. The car handled like a dream. The power was smooth

and solid, and I could steer the car anyplace I wanted
to go. It was fantastic.

The next day I ran a series of tests that went well
into the 300s. I decided that we were ready. We would
run for the record at daybreak on the third day. With
this, the newsmen rushed into town to the telephones
and did everything but yell, "Stop the presses," because they, too, felt that the record was about to return
to this country. Meanwhile, I helped the crew check
the car over and put it on the line at the north end of
the course.

I was a little nervous that night and went to bed
about nine o'clock. I always sleep well the night before
I race because I'm usually tired from the work and the
tension of the day. But almost without fail, I wake up in
the morning *scared*. I'm never sure what it is that's
scaring me, because I can never remember my dreams,
but I lie in bed in a cold sweat until I make out where I
am and what it is I'm supposed to be doing that day.
The night of August 5, 1963, was no exception to the
Craig Breedlove routine for racing.

Anyway, finally I got out of bed, went to the window,
and pulled back the drapes. It was still dark, but I
could see there were no clouds; so the prospects for
favorable weather were good. The neon lights along
Main Street illuminated the row of trees beside the
motel, and I could see that there was very little wind.
It would be a good day. I dressed and was lacing the
9,000 or so laces on my racing boots when Nye
knocked at the door. "Craig, you awake?" he said.

"Yeah, just a minute, Nye," I answered.

I opened the door and asked, "The rest of the guys
up yet?"

He looked at me and said, "Are you kidding?"

I guess it was a silly question. Every evening we
told the guys that we wanted them up by five, but

somehow they never got up. I suppose that we worked them too hard — or it might have been the late hours they spent at the State Line Casino. But they did have to have *some* relaxation, I suppose. Whatever the reason, as usual we knocked on all the doors and got the boys out of bed.

On race days I don't eat breakfast because I've convinced myself it's better to have an empty stomach in case I'm injured. This works out pretty well — I'm sure I couldn't keep anything down, anyway. It didn't take long to get ready to leave.

It was all so different. Before it had been complete turmoil for two weeks; in 1963 it was a three-day affair. We had practiced Sunday and Monday, and on Tuesday we were ready for the record run. Everything was perfect, and a few minutes after we reached the Flats, the car was uncovered and ready to go.

As I climbed up the ladder, I knew that it was for a purpose. There would be no more practice runs, no more uncertainty. We were *really* ready, and the British were about to lose their record. I eased into the cockpit and was ready as the first rays of sun spilled across Floating Mountain at the end of the Salt Flats. I looked at the mountain, which got its name from an obvious optical illusion, and it seemed as if it were flying instead of just floating.

"This must be a good omen," I thought.

The stop on the throttle was set at 85 percent power. I wanted things to move quickly because I knew everything was right and I wanted it over with.

In a few minutes the car was fired up and ready to go. I slammed the throttle to the stop, and the car blazed down the salt.

As the speed mounted, I was more relaxed and more aware of my surroundings than I had been on any earlier run. There was a certain speed at which the salt

spray off the tires powdered and the salt floated
through the inside of the cockpit, almost like smoke. It
floated around inside with me, and the tires began to
vibrate viciously, resonating, shaking the car. It was
pulsating resonance, and there was always a question
in my mind, "Is it something that will pass as the speed
builds or is there really something wrong?" This time
the vibration was gone in a few seconds and I felt as if
I was just sort of *on top* and moving. The *Spirit* was
really making it. It was a fantastic feeling. I was up and
planing and gone! I knew it.

I saw the timing lights come and go. Then I took a
deep breath from my mask and cut the power. I turned
off all the switches, put the chutes out, and got ready to
use the brakes once I got down to around 100 MPH. I
wanted to stop as quickly as possible so as not to drag
the chutes along abrasive salt surface any farther than
necessary. The speed dropped quickly, and I slowed
the car surely to a stop. Stan Goldstein came running
with an aluminum stepladder, and I released the canopy. He took it down the ladder, and I stepped out.

There were a lot of people waiting about, but I
didn't want to talk to newsmen or anybody until I had
made the second run. I told the crew to refuel the car
and turn it around because I wanted to go back as soon
as possible. The wind was starting to pick up, and that
would affect the car's handling.

USAC's Joe Petrali drove up and handed me the slip
of paper that told the speed — three hundred
eighty-eight miles an hour. I was a little disappointed;
I would need at least 412 on the return run. I climbed
the ladder and reset the stop on the throttle with a
screwdriver. Ninety percent power.

I slipped into the cockpit and put on my helmet. As
Nye helped me set the mask in place, he said, "This is
it, you know."

And I said, "Yeah, I know."

He tapped me on the top of the helmet and said, "Play it cool."

The run back was smooth. I entered the measured mile at well over 400, and the car was really flying when I left it. The air speed indicator pointed to 440 MPH. I knew I had it. I *knew* it. The average speed for the run would be about 425.

I couldn't wait to get the car stopped, so I could see the crew. We had all worked hard, and I was sure we had it. When I got out, someone said, "How fast, boss?"

I said, "About 425."

Everybody froze and waited for the official word.

When I saw Joe's face as he got out of the jeep, I knew that we were in. He put his arm around me and handed me the paper—*four hundred twenty-eight miles an hour!* And then the place broke up. Everybody was screaming and jumping and hugging each other, and it was a *great* feeling. Flash bulbs were going off all around, and about 20 newsmen were trying to interview me at the same time. All I could say was, "Oh, man, I've got the record! I've got the *record!*"

The *Spirit of America* had returned the world's land speed record to the United States for the first time since Ray Keech, the Indianapolis champion, had gone 207.55 MPH in 1928. My average for the two runs was 407.45 MPH.

Most of the crew went into town when things settled down a little, but I stayed at the Flats for about two hours being interviewed by the newsmen. By the time I got back to the motel, there was a wild party going on throughout the building—I mean *everyplace*—in the rooms, the lobby, the parking lot. There were even a couple of fellows on the roof. They deserved it.

When the crew saw me drive in, a cheer went up for the conquering hero. The Goodyear and Shell people were there, and they had planned a big dinner in Salt Lake City that night, to be attended by company officials, the crew, the USAC people, and newsmen.

When things had died down in the afternoon, I showered and dressed for the dinner, which turned out to be a gala affair at the rooftop gardens of the Hotel Utah.

Next morning I was on a plane to New York with a Goodyear public relations man for a television appearance on the Today and Tonight shows. Things were really happening too fast. I hardly had had time to think, and I really wanted to be with the crew. I never did have much time to sit down and talk with them, not even to thank them properly for making it all possible. Goodyear was talking about a nationwide tour after the New York TV appearance, and it was clear that I might not get to see them for two months or so. I hoped that they understood.

I also thought of my future. "What happens now? I've broken the record and it's all over. Now, what am I going to do for a job?" I wondered.

When I got to New York, I went to see Monty Spaight, president of Shell Oil. He was as happy as a kid about the record. He congratulated me on what he called "a magnificent job" and asked me to come back the next morning to talk with some of his people and with some Goodyear people who were flying in from Akron.

In the meantime, Vic Holt, Goodyear's executive vice-president, called to say that he would see me the next day at Shell's offices. He said, "This is the biggest racing victory we've ever had, Craig, and I can say for all of us here that we're mighty glad *you* didn't go across town that day you came to Akron." Rivalry between the two Akron tire giants, Goodyear and Firestone, whose plant is just across the city, is very acute!

Bob Lane, Goodyear's public relations director, met me at the hotel next morning, and we went over to the meeting at Shell. I was in for the biggest surprise of my life. The two companies had already met and decided what was in store for me.

Bill Lawler stood up and said, "Craig, we have an offer to make you, and we hope it's to your liking." At that stage I would have taken any offer because I was out of work. But the terms they talked of were astounding, to say the least. Each company was going to pay me $1,000 a month for three years as a racing consultant. I felt like kissing somebody, but fortunately I restrained myself and said, "That sounds fine to me, gentlemen. I'll be honored to work for Shell and Goodyear." What I wanted to say was, "I'll take it. Wow!"

The two companies first wanted me to make a nationwide tour, which would last three months. For this I would receive an additional $200 a day, plus $100 a day expenses. It was incredible—$2,000 a month plus travel expenses. For the first time in my life I would know what it feels like to have money. I had scrimped and saved every nickel and dime I had gotten since I was 13 and had wanted the coupe. I couldn't remember when I ever had money right there—without saving and saving—to buy anything I really wanted. The record had been important to me and I was proud of what I had done, but the money was like the biggest present in the world. I was just about knocked off my feet.

They said I could take Lee on the press tour, and I called her and told her the news. She was so happy she cried. We made plans for her to fly to New York to join me for the first leg of the tour. She would have to quit her job and, of course, that didn't break her heart. Our recently acquired affluence was something new for her, too. It meant not only money for us; it meant that she could spend some time with the kids for the first time. That's why she said she wanted to make the first month of the tour and then go back and stay with them.

The first appearance on the press tour was at the Americana Hotel in New York. A press conference was planned, and newsmen from all over the world would be there. Here I was—the guy who didn't even like to give book reports in English class—about to hold a press conference in one of New York's plushest hotels. The conference went on for three hours, and next day papers all over the world carried accounts of the interviews with the "All American Boy," a title I picked up after the record. I didn't know if I was Craig Breedlove or Jack Armstrong. The papers said I was clean-cut and polite and honest. I was flattered, but fortunately I had plenty of friends to make sure it didn't all go to my head.

The tour, which took me to 38 major American cities, was a grind. It was like a series of one-night stands. One of the public relations people would go to the next city a day ahead to beat the drums and set up the press conference. I would hit the town, do the conference, and then go from one television station to another for personal interviews. I told the same story at least six times a day. It was a great story and I meant every word of everything I said, but the pace was killing me: I went from 150 to 134 pounds. But I did become a proficient speaker. At first I was more frightened of the television cameras and radio microphones than I was of driving the jet car. Later I got used to them, and I kind of liked the public affairs, but I would have liked them more if they had been taken at a slower pace.

When the tour ended, Bob Lane told me that he felt that it had been an outstanding success. "You've done a great job, Craig. But we want you to do one more thing, if you can stand it. You wouldn't mind touring England and Australia, would you?" he asked.

Was he kidding? Before the tour, I had thought a trip to Akron, Ohio, was exciting. England and Australia—would I mind it! Suddenly, I wasn't tired anymore. I had never been any "real" place but the Salt Flats in my life until the jet car project, and I had always dreamed of travel. I even liked the press tour of the United States, despite the tremendous grind, because as a result I had seen, if only briefly, every major city in the nation.

The trip to England was superb. I went by ship and just rested—for six days. When I arrived, I was surprised to find that the English press was just as excited about my record as the American press had been —probably because of Britain's great LSR interest. After all, the British *had* held the record for 34 years, and traditionally, since the beginning of land speed racing, they had been dominant in that category. They treated me wonderfully and made me feel very important. I loved every minute in England.

The highlight of the trip came on my second day, when I met Donald Campbell, the British land and water speed king. Campbell had been a sort of hero to me for years, and he seemed a little unreal. I had never expected to meet him at all—let alone when *I* held the record and *he* was the challenger.

Campbell had not run since 1961, when he had crashed his car, *Bluebird*. He was receiving a lot of criticism because of that failure and because scores of British companies had put $4.5 million into the car. In fact, I was to Campbell what Glenn Leasher had been to me—a shoestring budget operation.

Anyway, I was finally going to meet my idol, and I was a little embarrassed. I remember driving out to his magnificent place in the country and thinking, "Why couldn't I have met him before the record? I hope he doesn't think I'm coming out here to show off." Well, I couldn't have been more wrong; he gave me the warmest greeting I could imagine. There were scores of newsmen there, and photographers were having a field day, taking photos of the old and the new regime of racers. Campbell had been trying for years to break the record that his father, Sir Malcolm Campbell, had once held; the young American had done it. The press was there to crucify the "old man."

The funny thing is, though, five minutes after we had all arrived, Campbell had everyone wrapped around his little finger, with his warm, gracious, English gentleman manner. He was spectacular. The press had expected excuses for his failures to break the record. Instead he praised me and joked with the press, completely at his ease. Nothing unflattering about Campbell appeared in any paper's coverage of the meeting. I was pleased; he had gotten to me, too. It was hard not to be trapped by his charm. At the beautiful buffet luncheon he had set up for me, he stood up and toasted me with champagne. It took a while to say, "Thank you, Donald," and when I did, my voice cracked. It isn't often that a hero becomes a friend.

Craig's pride and joy—the drag-racing coupe he built himself before he was old enough for a driver's license.

The flathead engine in the coupe that got Craig started racing. He began working on the car at age 13.

Craig's "belly-tank" lakester was made from a surplus World War II aircraft fuel tank.

Craig keeps a close eye on the progress charts for the *Spirit of America.*

The first jet car takes shape in the Breedlove garage.

Craig in the role of welder as the jet car goes together in his garage.

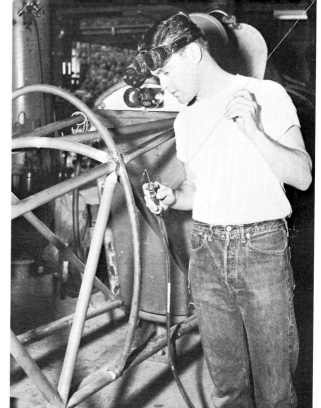

The air intake ducts were formed in Craig's living room. Each was 10 feet long and weighed about 300 pounds

Robert D. K.

Wind-tunnel testing proved a three-wheeled design was aero-dynamically best for the speeds Craig was attempting.

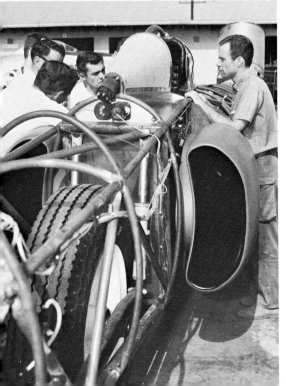

The jet car leaves the garage for its trip to the body shop.

Getting the 11½-foot-wide car out of the garage and down the driveway presented obstacles: the fence, the porch, and Mr. Tuchen's hedge.

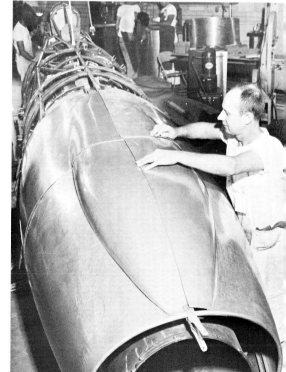

Quinn Epperly fits the body to the 40-foot *Spirit of America*.

Craig revs up the jet engine for a test firing at Los Angeles
International Airport.

Crew members marvel at one of the *Spirit of America* 48-inch
tires and wheels.

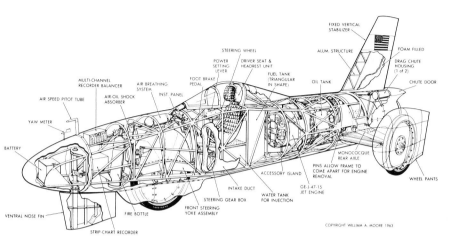

Schematic drawing of the three-wheeled *Spirit of America* jet car.

Craig and crew get the car ready for a shot at the record.

Chute-maker Jack Carter packs a chute into its housing as part of the braking system.

The *Spirit of America* arrives at the Salt Flats in 1962.

The jet car is towed to the firing line.

A confident Craig Breedlove strides away from a practice run.

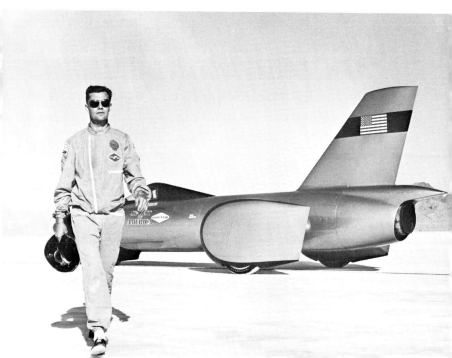

The *Spirit of America* looks at home on the Salt Flats.

The world's land speed record returns to the United States as Craig Breedlove averages 407.45 MPH on August 5, 1963.

Joe Petrali, USAC official, second from right, gives Craig his record time.

Craig Breedlove celebrates his new world's land speed record.

Craig embarks on the ride that made him, in 1964, the first man to travel over 500 MPH in a car.

"The wildest ride" ends in 18 feet of salt water after setting a new record of 526.27 MPH.

Alive to enjoy his new record, Craig talks to newsmen as his car sinks slowly in the west.

A crew member weeps when he finds Craig still alive after the crash.

Cockpit of the *Spirit of America* before and after the 1964 crash into the briny lake.

Craig inspects the damage after the jet car had been hauled back onto the salt.

Co-driver Bobby Tatroe helps Craig get ready for his crack at the circular course at the Flats.

Crew chief Nye Frank, second from right, oversees the running of the Daytona coupe at the Salt Flats.

Walt Arfons' first *Wingfoot Express*, driven by Tom Green, captures the world's land speed record.

The second *Wingfoot Express:* the Rocket Car.

Art Arfons sets a world's land speed record in his Green Monster in 1965. Craig Breedlove topped it a week later.

The late Donald Campbell before his try for the record in the *Bluebird.*

Stuart Per

Campbell inspects th*e Bluebird* before his 403-MPH run.

Stuart Per

Craig talks with his most loyal supporter: his dad.

Craig inspects brake damage following a ride in the *Spirit of America—Sonic I* when the chutes failed.

The business end of *Spirit*, showing chute housings, lower right and left.

A dejected Craig Breedlove walks away from the *Spirit of America—Sonic I* after near tragedy.

The *Spirit of America—Sonic 1* poised to take the world's land speed record.

(Above) The *Spirit of America—Sonic I* fires up for its record run of 600.601 MPH on November 15, 1965. (Below) The *Spirit* nears the measured mile covering nearly one mile every five seconds.

(Above) Chutes help Breedlove slow down after traversing the measured mile. (Below) The *Spirit* comes to a stop after setting a new world's land speed record.

Craig and his wife Lee broke 106 national and international records in this AMX.

Craig poses with his newest dragster, *American Spirit*, which is designed to go 300 MPH.

11.   The Brothers Arfons

Life to me was bright and warm while I rested in England — at first. The evenings were filled with parties and dinners, and I felt like a foreign head of state. I wouldn't have been surprised to have been introduced: "And here he is, my lords, ladies, and gentlemen — the Imperial Potentate, His Majesty King Craig the First, Lord of All He Surveys, Ruler of the Land Known as the Kingdom of Salt, Population: One."

The introductions were far simpler, fortunately, and I was usually presented as "Craig Breedlove, the fastest man on wheels."

So the first days were beautiful and I was impressed with the warm reception I received everywhere.

Then things got complicated. The Fédération Internationale Motorcycliste (FIM) presented me with a gold medal for my accomplishment. This award was noted in the British press and prompted the Fédération Internationale Automobile (FIA), the other world speed record sanctioning body, to put out a press release saying that they had not *certified* the record. All the release was meant to do was to straighten out a few confused newspapers that had referred to the gold medal as an FIM award. Instead, the release muddled the whole issue, and papers all over the world misunderstood. A lot of papers now said that the record wasn't official. This brought a few comments like, "It's not a record. Anybody can put a jet engine on a tricycle and go 400 miles an hour." My feelings were really hurt, so I was very glad when that evening I had the opportunity on a BBC television interview, to explain the world record situation. Then I answered the few criticisms of the run by saying—nationwide, mind you—"Next year I plan to go back to the Salt Flats and go 500 miles an hour."

The papers really played up my boast, and next day I thought, "Well, the loudmouthed kid has done it again."

Overall the tour was pleasant, but I got a little tired of doing nothing but resting during the day, speaking at night, and then going to bed. For days I did nothing else, as I mentioned to Tom Gaylen, president of the United States Motorcycle Club, who was at one of the dinners.

He said, "You mean nobody has taken you out on the town in London yet?"

"The only thing I have seen is the inside of a hotel room and about 6,000 formal dining rooms," I answered.

He was appalled. "Well, tonight, Craig, my boy," he said, "you'll see what London night life is like."

I was really excited because I had never even seen what *Los Angeles* night life was like. That evening we met a South African motorcycle champion named Reggie Dyvers, and the three of us drove to a remote spot on the outskirts of London. It was a pretty dark section of the city, and I thought to myself, "Is this what they call night life?" What was wrong with Piccadilly Circus or somewhere with people?

Eventually we arrived at a place called Murray's Club, Ltd., and when I got inside, I couldn't believe it. The place was mobbed. It was the wildest spot I had ever seen. The club had a chorus line that would have

put Las Vegas and the Rockettes to shame, and I just
stood there in awe. We were seated right near the
stage, and Tom and Reggie were ordering champagne
and hors d'oeuvres like they were going out of style. I
ate a few of the snacks and tasted the champagne, but I
wasn't much of a drinker; so I just sat and watched the
chorus line.

Somehow word got to the management that Craig
Breedlove was in the audience. I was introduced and I
again felt like the toast of the town.

Then Tom got a phone call and said that he had to
leave for an hour or so, but for us to wait right there as
he would be back. However, after an hour or so, Reggie
got tired of waiting and disappeared. The last show was
over.

The club stayed open until 4:00 A.M. — even though
the last show had ended at two — and I sat there until
closing time, drinking orange juice and talking to the
bartender about land speed racing — the one thing I had
wanted to get away from for an evening. Then the
waitress brought me the check. I looked at it and it
didn't mean anything to me, just a lot of pounds and
shillings.

"How much is this in dollars?" I asked the bartender.

He figured it out and told me, "One hundred for-
ty-four."

I gulped and said, "That's just great. I've never paid
$144 to drink orange juice before." To make matters
worse, it had probably been California orange juice.

Fortunately, I had converted some American money
at the hotel before I left for the evening — $150 worth.
The change wouldn't even amount to a decent tip, but
I gave it to the waitress, anyway. It was all I had. I
walked out into the blackest, foggiest night I had ever
seen and onto the darkest, most deserted street — dead

broke. I thought, "The toast of the town, are you?" There wasn't a car in sight; so I started walking. At least the bartender had told me in which direction to head.

After a few blocks, I saw a policeman and told him of my problem. He walked me over to a busier street and hailed a cab. "Take this 'ere gentleman to the De Vere Hotel and 'e'll arrange for payment when 'e arrives," he said. We got to the hotel at about five in the morning. The doors were locked. Finally, after what seemed like an age, during which I nearly smashed in the door, a man appeared dressed in a Fisk uniform, with stocking cap and nightgown (the only thing he didn't have was the tire over his shoulder and the candle). He grumbled, but he did let me in. I told him my problem and he pondered it for a while, then went to the desk and advanced me the exact fare for the cabbie—no tip, just the exact fare. The cabbie growled and drove away, and I just stood there. Some night on the town that had been!

I left later that day for Australia and was impressed with the crowd of people who greeted me at the airport. My two weeks in that country were a wonderful experience. The people were robust and happy-go-lucky, and I felt at home. The Australians, too, have a strong interest in the land speed record because Donald Campbell has made a few of his runs there on Lake Eyre, the Australian Salt Flats.

Finally the tour ended. It was August, 1964, and, despite the good time I had in England and Australia, I was anxious to get home. I knew my competition was getting ready, and I wanted to know what was going on.

I had good reason to be worried. The tremendous

publicity surrounding the breaking of the record had stirred up a lot of activity, particularly in Akron, Ohio, where both Walt Arfons and his brother Art were completing cars for an assault on the record.

The two brothers had not been on friendly terms for several years; so their entry into the race constituted a serious threat. They would be trying to beat *each other* as well as me, and I knew this was exactly the incentive to make them go fast—as if they needed any extra incentive!

Earlier I had rented a large garage and the *Spirit* stood ready, but I called Nye Frank and asked him to bring me up to date on the two cars. He had been watching the situation.

"They're really serious, Craig, and they've got some good backing. Walt is about ready to go with the *Wingfoot Express,* and Art isn't far behind with the *Green Monster,*" Nye said.

"You know they're mad at each other, and that's going to make them try even harder," he added.

"I know. I've already thought of that. We'd better get Walt Sheehan and some of the fellows, and take a look at the *Spirit* to see what modifications and refinements it might need," I said.

Within a day we got word that Walt had left Akron and was on his way to the Salt Flats. We would have to hustle, and the first step was to get on a plane in Los Angeles so that I would be able to see what the competition looked like. In all of my racing encounters, I've always been interested in watching other people run against my records. I feel that I can do a better job if I know exactly what I'm competing against, and the only way I can be sure I know what is coming up is to see it myself. I study my competitors' machinery, their technique, and, most of all, their courage. You have to know how brave your opponent is if you expect to be braver.

I knew the Arfons brothers wouldn't waste much time on the Flats. They would be in and out in nothing flat, whether or not they had the record. That's the way they operate. Walt and Art have their shops side by side in Akron and work in exactly the same manner. Their cars are sometimes a little crude, but they usually go fast.

Most of the Arfonses' running before 1964 had been done on drag strips, and I was familiar with their creations. On one of my trips to Akron I had even visited their shops and was amazed with what I saw. They had a bunch of old jet airplanes out back that they had bought from some surplus outlet. When they needed an instrument or a part, they would just go out back with a hacksaw or a welding torch, cut it out, and bolt it on the new car. Even though they were side by side, their operations were completely independent, and each had his own private collection of wrecked airplanes.

Their cars had been used at drag strips as drawing cards. Their creations are the ones you hear about on the radio or see on television: "See the world's fastest dragsters battle it out as fire blazes from the tail of two jet-powered race cars. Yes, sir, see it right here tomorrow night!" But they drew the people, and the cars turned well into the high 200s on the quarter-mile strips. The crowds loved them.

Walt's new car, the *Wingfoot Express*, was pretty much like his drag cars, except it was larger. It was powered by a J-46, but it also was fitted with an afterburner. Both brothers had plenty of afterburner experience from their drag strip runs. The burner was used at the strips because it gave the jet engine a quicker burst of power, which was needed for the short sprints. The burner also caused more fire to shoot out of the tail, making the crowd cringe with excitement.

The simplified principle of a jet engine is this: the air enters the front of the engine and is pumped rearward by a series of rotary and stationary blades. The rotary blades are attached to a cone-shaped hub, and as the air moves toward the rear, it is squeezed against the outer compressor case where the stationary blades are fixed. The compressed air is then forced into a combustion chamber where fuel is injected and ignited. The hot expanded gases then pass through a series of blades connected to the turbine wheel, which causes the wheel to spin with tremendous force. The turbine wheel is connected to the cone-shaped center of the compressor which got the whole process started in the first place. The hot exhaust gases then are forced out of the tail pipe of the engine with phenomenal velocity. This velocity pushes the plane or car forward. On an engine with an afterburner (and these are primarily military aircraft, which often have to take off on short runways and need the extra push), additional fuel is sprayed on the escaping jet blast just before it exits and is reignited. The technical name for an afterburner is a "re-heat section." It's just a raw flame explosion at the last instant before the jet stream hits the outside air.

Well, the Arfonses had plenty of experience with burners, and I had none. I had felt that I didn't need a burner—it would be just another thing that could go wrong—so I hadn't put a burner on the *Spirit*.

When I arrived at the Salt, Walt Arfons and I sat down and talked for a long time. His men were getting his car ready for a practice run, and he intended to go for the record as soon as possible. There would be no fooling around. Walt is a perfect gentleman, the kind of person I like to be around. He's soft-spoken and always has something nice to say to everybody. But he doesn't mess around.

"Craig," he said, "my car doesn't look as nice as yours, but I think it's going to be pretty fast."

I looked at the car and said, "Yes, sir, it does look fast."

"I know you've worked hard for the record and I really hate to take it away from you so soon," Walt added, "but if I don't, Art's going to be right up here whacking away at it, and I don't want that."

I could only say, "I understand, Walt, and I'll be right back whacking away at both of you."

He laughed and said, "You wouldn't be much of a champion if you didn't, would you?"

The question didn't need an answer.

Walt was unable to drive because he had suffered a heart attack a few months earlier and his doctor made him retire from driving; so Tom Green, one of his friends, was going to drive the car. Tom had some interest in the LSR and had helped Walt design and build the car. Tom had given Walt some ideas and researched the aerodynamic aspect of the design.

Tom made a run the first day, and the car went straight and fast—about 350 MPH. It looked like the record, for which I had worked so hard, was going to fall. Walt told Joe Petrali that Tom would be ready to run the car at daybreak.

I went up on top of the mountain that overlooks the motel that night and sat for a long time. I had gone there before; it was a perfect place to get away from all distractions and to think. At first there were no sounds except those of the rental car I had brought from Salt Lake City. It cracked and creaked softly as the hot metal parts cooled and contracted. In a minute there

was no sound at all, except the drone of disappointment that raced through my heart and my head.
I knew that my record was going to be broken. But
soon the sounds within me stopped, too, because they
ran headlong into determination. I stood and shouted
out into the darkness: "I'll get it back! I'll get it back!"

By the first sign of daylight, Tom was in the car and
ready to go. His first run averaged 408 MPH; his run
back was 421. His average was 413 MPH—he was the
holder of the world's land speed record. I congratulated Walt and Tom, posed for a bunch of photos
of the three of us, and went back to the motel. I drove
right into my second shock of the day.

There in the parking lot of the Wendover Motel sat
the *Green Monster*. Art Arfons was wiping it off. As I
parked my car, I asked myself, "Just why did you get
out of bed today?"

I walked over and shook hands with Art. "Heard the
news?" I asked.

"Yeah, Craig, sorry about your record," Art said.

"That's okay, Walt said *you* would have done it if he
hadn't," I said.

He looked at me with a twinkle in his eye and said,
"Now what made him say a thing like that?"

Art is different from Walt. He's more outgoing and
jovial. He, too, is genuine, but he's a tougher competitor. I was sure he would be the one I would have to
struggle with longest. Then I looked at the car, and I
knew that he would be the tougher competitor. It *was* a
monster. Big and burly-looking, it was powered by a
J-79 engine from an F-104 fighter. It had 17,000 pounds
of thrust—more than three times that of the *Spirit*. I
just looked at it and shook my head.

"It really looks strong, Art," I said.

"It is, Craig," Art answered.

It was clear that the car was not as streamlined as
mine, but with power like that Art would be able to
break the record driving the motel building.

There was no doubt that Art would break the record,
and after I had watched the car in the practice run next
day, I packed my gear. I had to go home and get ready.
My work was cut out for me.

Two days later Art averaged 434 MPH and broke
Walt's three-day-old record. I was now third on a list of
"fastest men on wheels," and I was determined not to
stay there any longer than necessary.

When the news arrived, we had already started to
work around the clock on a few modifications, most of
which involved reshaping the nose of the car a little to
give it an even more streamlined design. We went over
the car with a fine-toothed comb to see if we could
improve it *anyplace*. We cut down the front steering fin
and reshaped some of the fillets. The wind tunnel test
had proven that the shape of the car was nearly perfect.
So we tightened and polished and tuned and, well, just
nervously fiddled around.

Clyde Schetter, Goodyear's public relations man in
Los Angeles, called and said, "Do you know Art went
479 on his return run? He averaged 434, but he went
479 on the last run—four hundred seventy-nine! What
are *your* plans?"

I said, "Yeah, Clyde, I know. Art's not fooling around
and I'm really impressed with his speed, but I'm not
fooling around either. You can tell the press that I've
made a lot of modifications to the car. I'm still going to
go 500."

I told the fellows to load the car; we would leave
that night for the Flats. Then I called Lee and told her
I had to leave right away.

All she said was, "Yes, I've been expecting your call.
Clyde called here first, thinking you would be at home,

and told me the news. Do you want me to go with you?"

I said, "No, I think it would be better if you stayed here with the kids. They might need you."

She could tell that I was concerned about the run and said, "Okay, but call me the minute you get there."

I sat down in the office of the garage and collected my thoughts. I hoped that the tour had not gotten me too far out of condition. I usually work out in a gym every day when I'm at home because I feel that it's important to keep in shape physically as well as mentally, and I certainly had had no time for that sort of thing while on tour. At least I felt up to the strain mentally, and mental strength is the most important factor when you're driving at the phenomenal rates of speed that the LSR demands. You really have to be up on it. Your reactions have to be sharp; your mind has to zing. It has to be clear. Massive quantities of information pour through it, as if it was a computer.

I thought of how difficult it had been to run 400. It now had to be 500 — 500 over the tire ruts Walt and Art had made in the race course. The ruts had been bad after Walt's record runs and Art's practice runs; they could only have become worse from Art's runs. The *Spirit* was difficult to steer through ruts because of its three-wheeled configuration. If the front wheel got into a rut, it might be like riding down the street on a motorcycle and getting caught in streetcar tracks. In fact, the car tended to follow ruts even though they were only an inch or so deep. There were a lot of ruts on the Flats now.

In the final analysis, however, none of these things mattered. The Salt Flats belonged to me and I was going up there to get my record back.

12. The Loud-Mouthed Kid Strikes Back

Driving a race car across the ground at 400 MPH is a scary thing. It's a ride you don't forget; so, despite my determination, as we pulled into Wendover, I had some mental reservations. Chiefly I thought, "And you've said you'll add another 100 miles to the record. Nice play, loudmouth."

Tom Green had taken the rational approach after Art had broken his record. Tom said, "That's enough of this stuff for me. I can say I held the land speed record at one time, and if you guys want to mess around with this Russian roulette stuff, go ahead, but let me off the merry-go-round. This is insanity."

Tom had one advantage over me, however. He was not committed. For me, there could be no backing off; so when we arrived in Wendover, I just checked into the motel, and the guys took the car and the equipment to the Flats. It was too late to run that day, but the crew could get the camp set up and the car off the trailer. Doing things kept my mind busy, but as soon as I had time to myself, I had to face my thoughts, which, at least as I sat in my room, involved wondering where it was all going to end. It wasn't just a matter of breaking the record anymore. Suddenly I had competition—competition with three times the power I had, I might add—and I was feeling the pressure. Before, my concern had been to get the car ready, keep the crew busy, watch the weather, and run for the record. Now I had to keep the wolves off my back. I wasn't too happy about the idea that I would have to go out there and run every time somebody felt like breaking my record. I remembered too well what it was like out there, having that big car sliding around, bouncing and banging. Yes, I had misgivings, but that didn't make any difference. I was in Wendover. My car was running. "My" record had been taken from me. I had to try to get it back.

I decided to drive out to the course. As I drove up to the camp, I smelled the aroma of the Salt Flats — hot dogs cooking on a grill, jet fuel being pumped into the car, coffee heating on a hot plate. It was just the same as last year, only I had lost a lot of the enthusiasm for the whole thing. Now I was there of necessity.

Next day I ran the car about 300 MPH. The condition of the track was even worse than I had thought, compounding my concern about the whole affair. The Arfons's cars had really chewed up the salt, and it was difficult to keep the *Spirit* in a straight line. But I had little choice if I intended to live up to my promise. And, as if I wasn't determined enough, Art had told the *Akron Beacon Journal* that I would never go 500. I would just have to find the smoothest portions of the track and try to steer around the rough spots. I was going to go 500.

On the next practice run I certainly didn't find the smooth route. At about 400 MPH, I hit a series of bumps, and the car went up on two wheels — off course and heading, as I later learned, straight for Joe Petrali's timing shack. I shut the engine down, got the car back on the course and popped the chutes. I was too busy to notice at the time that the car was headed for Joe's shack, but I was told that Joe's eyes were as big as the 48-inch tires on the *Spirit*. So were mine.

Discovering the proper route was going to take time.

I walked the course, drove it in an automobile, and did everything but crawl it on my hands and knees (I would have done that if I had thought it would help). Finally, I felt that I knew every inch, soft spot, and rut—and there was no way to miss them all. All I could do was select a relatively smooth course and memorize it. Now, if I just had a navigator with a road map so that I wouldn't forget the route, everything would be fine. Unfortunately, I couldn't get a taker. He would have had to ride outside.

The following morning I decided to make a try at a record run. The weather was good, and the track would only get worse. The car was ready. The south end of the course was the roughest; so I decided to run through it first, building up speed as I approached the smooth, measured mile. I went only 438, but I expected the first to be the slower run because the build-up had to be made through the bumpy end of the course. On the return trip I would have to shut down in the rough portion, but by then I would already be through the mile.

The trip back was frightening. I was really blazing as I left the measured mile. As I cut the engine and hit the parachute button—the small dynamite charge that fires the pilot chute popped loud and clear—I hit the rough stuff with such force that my head smashed right through the side of the plexiglass canopy. Luckily, my head bounced right back in, and I held tightly to the steering wheel as the car bounced to a stop. The entire right side of the canopy had been smashed out, and my racing helmet bore deep scars. I had a headache, but I again held the world's land speed record. The average speed of the two runs was 468 MPH. The return run was 498, a heartbreaking 2 MPH off the 500 I had said I would do.

Thus I faced another grueling series of runs, for I

was going to go 500. We spent the next day repairing the canopy and installing rubber pads in the cockpit, so that when I was thrown around, I would at least be bouncing off cushions, not metal. Once the cockpit was padded and the canopy repaired, I went over to talk to Roland Portwood, who was in charge of the road crew that was maintaining the track. As I rode up and down on the truck, I saw that his guys were really doing their best to get the course smooth. They couldn't do the impossible, but it was good to see they were doing all they could.

Track conditions for LSR attempts are not what most people think. Chuck holes, and even a two-foot wide ditch, don't affect the handling of the car because it's traveling at such fantastic speeds. At 500 MPH you are approaching at 900 feet per second (which, incidentally, is faster than a .45 caliber bullet travels). At that speed the suspension doesn't even have time to react as it passes over a hole. If a wheel goes over a one-foot-diameter hole, it is over it only for one nine-hundredth of a second. The wheel just doesn't have time to drop. It drops maybe one-sixteenth of an inch before there's something solid under it again. If you drive down the LSR course in a stock car at 100 MPH, you notice the holes, but not in the jet car at 400 or 500 MPH.

A change in the elevation of the course is a different thing, however. A six-inch drop in one mile is equivalent to running off a curb in a regular car because you cover the ground so quickly. The jet car is traveling so fast that slight changes in elevation are crucial and can have a significant effect on LSR attempts. Yet it's almost impossible to remove these particular irregularities from the course with normal road grading equipment, and this is all that's available at the Flats.

Roland and his crew were doing everything possible,

and I stayed with them until midnight. I couldn't stay longer because I had to get some rest before the drive in the morning. They stayed all night, working on their own time to try to get that course ready for me.

I was really afraid of the run, but I felt that I had to make it if I wanted to keep Art off my back for the rest of the season. If I could just go 500, I felt that Art would not come back again at least until next year. Winning the LSR had suddenly become much more than a race. It had become a psychological battle, and I had started using a lot of strategy. Holding, not just winning, the LSR more and more involved psyching out the other guy. It's a super-dangerous thing, this running 500 MPH, and, somehow, I had to get Art thinking that there was no point in risking his car against the odds. I had to make Art think he was beat and keep him back in Akron for the winter.

That night, for the first time in my racing career, I couldn't sleep. I was tired, it was late, but I just lay in bed and tossed. I was afraid of the run next day, and I imagined the worst possible outcome. I feared the *Spirit* would not make it through the day, and I was sure that I would not see another sunset on the Salt Flats. I got up and wrote letters to my kids — nothing maudlin, just short notes to tell them that I was thinking of them on the night before my 500 MPH run and that I missed them. The tour and getting the car ready to run again had kept me away from them for the past six months, and I really did miss them. I called them often, but now it was too early in the morning to call. So I wrote to them instead.

I slept a little after writing the letters, and it was a badly needed rest. The next day was to be a big one.

13.

The Wildest Ride

A shiver ran through me as I stepped into the cold predawn air at the motel. I had awakened more scared than usual that morning, and the feeling had stayed with me. It was usually gone by the time I got out of bed, but this morning it rode with me to the Salt Flats. It was October 15, 1964. The air was crisp and clear, and there was little wind. The season was nearing its end.

Most of the crew and the newsmen were already at the Flats when Nye and I arrived. There were the usual greetings: "How's everything?" "What's happening?" "How do you feel, Craig?" But I wasn't in a mood to be sociable—even to talk, for that matter. There had been complete silence in the car on the way to the course because I had the run on the rough salt on my mind—500 MPH on the rough salt. Everybody was talking to me, and I muttered something noncommittal—"Fine," or something—and thought to myself, "I wish they'd just shut up and leave me alone so I can go out and do this."

We planned to use the same strategy as the day before. I would build up through the rough stuff on the first run and shut down in it on the way back. The car was ready at the south end of the course, and I walked over to it and mounted the ladder. I got in and rechecked the power setting. It was set at 97.5 percent power. I shivered again as I sat down. In the mornings the seat is always ice cold. The cockpit is stark.

I looked at my gloved hand. It was steady as a rock. My knees weren't shaking, but there was fear. It was an entirely different feeling from what I had experienced that time at El Mirage. Then it had been a fear of anticipation, of not really knowing what it's going to be like, a sort of nervousness. This time it was a fear for my life — and that's a lot different. I experienced a physical calmness, a strong, positive feeling, but I had a sensation new to me in the pit of my stomach — a tight feeling. I took a deep breath and felt a little better.

The routine process of getting the car ready momentarily took my mind off the fear. Each time I ran through the same checklist and flipped the same switches. It's like starting an airplane; you make doubly sure everything is ready. During the light-up procedure, you have to regulate the fuel pressure very carefully. It's a touchy situation, one that can easily be blown. If you flood the engine and blow the light-up, you have to wait 45 minutes for the next attempt at starting because of all the raw fuel in the chambers. And if you have to wait that long, you may have also blown the weather situation. So there's always pressure when you light the engine, but getting started is such a complicated process that I usually forget everything else. This time concentrating helped, but it didn't entirely eliminate my uneasiness. Still I was more settled and calm. As usual, I figured that I was commited.

With the engine started, I put my breathing mask on. Again everything was mechanical. There was a valve on the mask with which to adjust the flow of air, and I set it so that a little bit of oxygen was blowing on my face, even when I wasn't breathing. It cooled my mouth and my nose underneath the mask, and it was a refreshing feeling—a little like splashing my face with cold water. I felt a little sharper. I polished my goggles on the sleeve of my driving suit and looked at the windshield. It, of course, was clean, but I like to check everything.

The engine was idling. Everything was set to go. I looked at Nye and nodded, and he lowered the canopy. I pulled it down and jiggled it into place. I had sat in the car so often that putting the canopy on was like putting on an old jacket. I knew exactly how much to the right or left it had to be moved before the pins lined up and it dropped into place. Nye moved away and held up two fingers to remind me of the final two procedures: turn on the cameras that photograph the run, and turn on the electronic device—a photosensitive tape recorder that requires development of the tapeline film—that records the effects on the car, the pressure on the wheels, and the air speed. Both types of record are necessary for further developments of the car and for planning future LSR attempts.

I gave Nye the sign back, meaning, "Yeah, I remember," and planted two fingers on the respective switches. I was in go position. My hands held the wheel tightly, and my thumbs were right over the two parachute buttons mounted on the butterfly-type wheel—like gun buttons in World War II fighter planes.

I looked at the new foot throttle we had recently installed. Now, no matter what happened, I wouldn't have to take my hands off the wheel. The stop was set on the throttle, so all I had to do was slam the pedal down all the way and I would have the power setting we had planned on.

I took a deep breath and slammed the throttle to the floor. The car shot forward. It accelerated swiftly, and I was already doing over 400 MPH when I saw the rough stuff coming. I carefully maneuvered as far to the left side of the course as possible until I saw the marker for mile three flash by. Then I steered the car back to the right to avoid the next series of bumps. It bounced a little, but nothing like the day before. Roland and his men had done a good job.

As the car approached the measured mile, it was really moving. The needle on the air-speed indicator was nearing 500 MPH, and the car was streaking across the smooth salt like a comet. Clearing the second set of timing lights, I cut the engine.

Popping the chutes at such speeds is an unnerving experience. The deceleration forces from the fantastic speed affect your equilibrium in such a way that the earth seems to tilt. All of a sudden you seem to be running straight down the side of a cliff. It's as if the earth really *is* flat and you've run right off the edge of it. Then, as the car slows down, the earth "rights itself" and everything is in proper alignment again, but for a moment or two you hang on to the wheel extra tight.

The *Spirit* came to an easy stop, and the crew and newsmen rushed over. Bill Fleming of ABC's "Wide World of Sports" ran over to me and asked how it had felt. I said, "I'm sorry, Bill, but I can't talk to you right now. I have another run to make before it's official. I'll be happy to talk to you at the other end." He understood, and I told the crew to get the car ready for the return.

Joe Petrali drove up and handed me the paper. I had made the world's first 500 MPH run. The average speed was 513.33 MPH. I remember thinking, "That's a lucky number; there are a lot of threes in it."

The crew rapidly refueled the car, repacked the chutes, and checked everything—car and tires and *ev-*

erything. Then when I was ready to relight the engine, I was even more nervous. I knew that if I blew it now, the whole run was down the drain because I would not be able to make the required second run within the one-hour time limit. In any case, before we started the procedure, I leaned forward, removed the stop on the throttle, and tossed it to Nye. He kissed it and put it in his pocket. The run would be at 100 percent power — flat out.

The engine started, and I breathed a sigh of relief. I left the starting line with a feeling of confidence and didn't anticipate any rough salt. I swept past mile two at 450 MPH. And then it happened!

I heard a loud snap, and the car started pulling badly to the right. Frantically, I turned the wheel to the left. The car came back on course, but I had the steering wheel turned completely upside down. I didn't know whether to abort the run or to stay with it and hope for the best. I dimly realized that I must have lost one of the suspension bolts and that the front wheel was beginning to camber over. I was steering the car as if it were a motorcycle, and it was starting to lean. I could see the measured mile and I didn't know what to do, but I was moving so fast that I didn't have time to make a real decision, anyway. I was committed. I hadn't even taken my foot off the throttle. Then I was in the measured mile. All I could do was hang on to see if I could hack it through the timing lights.

The car started to lean more and more, getting off course again. I was convinced that it wasn't going to make the lights. In a flash I became afraid the car might hit one of the batteries used to power the lights; so I backed off the engine. The car immediately seemed to right itself; it was as if some kind of torque had been released, allowing it to go straight again.

Then it hit me that I could make the lights. I smashed down again on the throttle, and the engine caught and relit. With a big burst of speed, the car cleared the last marker under full power.

I glanced at my air speed. The needle was pointing to 550 MPH. Great! But the most important thing, at that point, was getting the car shut down. I was praying when I cut the power and hit the first chute button. I heard it fire and felt a tug: I knew I had lost my chute. I tried to collect my thoughts and actually talked out loud to myself. "You're going too fast, you've got to slow down." Mile four went by. "Wait just one more mile." I saw the sign for mile three and fired the emergency chute button. The gun went off, the sound reverberating inside the cockpit like a cannon—and there was nothing. No tug, nothing. The emergency chute must have come out with the first one and have been ripped off with it. I punched the button again and again. "You heard the gun go off, dummy. It's not going to fire again."

I knew that if I stepped on the brakes at that speed, they would just burn out; they had been designed for stopping at speeds of 150 MPH and less. I looked at the brake pedal and then at my air speed—the car was still going almost 500. I thought, "It's the only system you have left. If you don't step on the brakes now, it's going to be all over anyway." So I pressed the pedal. It smashed right to the floor. I pumped it again and again, and I could hear the sickening thud of the pedal hitting the metal floor. I had absolutely no brakes. I leaned back hard in the seat. I didn't know what to do, and I was still really traveling. I flashed by mile zero, where the car would normally have come to an easy stop. The crew and the newsmen stood by the marker, frozen in horror. I looked at my speed—420 MPH—and I was at the end of the course. Beyond the zero marker lay rough salt, a row of telephone poles, a shallow lake, and a ten-foot-high salt dike that had been built when a drainage ditch had been dug across the south end of the Flats.

Andy Linden, the ex-Indy driver, had once said, when he told of his car spinning out at 170 MPH at Monza, Italy, "You're apt to lose your balance if you step out at that speed." I could hear Andy's voice saying it as the rough salt loomed ahead.

There was nothing else left to look for outside. The markers were all gone; I would just have to ride it out. Suddenly, I seemed to have plenty of time. I looked at the roll bar and at all of the welds I had made in the car, and I remembered putting all of these things in. I glanced down at the instrument panel and remembered drilling the holes and mounting all of the instruments, forming all the metal support structures, and bending the windshield around. I looked at the padding put in to protect me, and I knew that I was trapped. I took a deep breath, and the oxygen rushed into my lungs. It was almost like being trapped in an iron lung.

I looked around the inside of my goggles and then refocused my eyes on the blue plexiglass of the windshield. I listened. The engine was shut down, and I could hear only the slamming and banging of the suspension as the car sped over the rough salt surface beneath it. I thought of the many times I had sat in the car. This was to be the last. I remembered all of the cars I had sat in and for a second thought of the black leather seats in the coupe. I distinctly remember asking myself: "What put me in this thing? Why am I here in the first place?"

I looked out of the windshield and gasped. Straight ahead was the row of telephone poles. I knew that I couldn't miss them, but I thought that if I could at least get the nose between two of them it might not be as bad. I steered to the right, and the car moved over a little. Then I put my head down ready for the impact, but there were only two sounds: WHACK! WHACK! The car was jarred a little, but it was still moving, and I thought, "I've got another chance."

Then the car hit the shallow salt lake, and the spray shot high into the air. The water was slowing the car down a little and it was a good feeling. But then I saw the dike looming straight in front of me. The car hit the dike and shot into the air—the whole horizon turned sideways. As the car cleared the top, the right outrigger wheel clipped the dike—just enough to give the car a tip—and the impact righted the car. It was flying like an airplane—level and straight and quiet. There wasn't a sound. Man, I was flying.

The horizon was gone and everything was crazy to me. Then the nose started to dip, and I could see the water under me. The car was going to land in the lake on the other side of the dike. All I could think of was getting the canopy off. I knew I wouldn't be able to get it off once the car was underwater; so I grabbed the latches and turned. The canopy popped up about two inches, and the wind pulled it out of my hands.

The car was almost in the water; so I tucked my hands inside my shoulder harness to hold my stomach because I knew that I was going to hit pretty hard. Then the car came down, with a tremendous crash, but broke free again, skipping across the water like a pebble. The next time the car hit, there was a big wall of water; only this time it was up over my head. The car was underwater. I snapped open the harness and started to climb out. I pulled about two or three times and couldn't get out of the car, and I thought, "Oh, no, all of this and now I'm going to drown." I started to panic but caught myself and said, "Just wait. There's something wrong, and you can figure it out."

The breathing mask, of course—it was still connected. I ripped it off the helmet, floated to the surface of the lake, and swam to the shore. I climbed out and stood there, looking at the car—its tail pipe sticking out of the water, weird sounds coming out of it. The water was steaming and going PLUNK, PLOP, GURGLE. I looked at my hands and my fingers and my feet. I was all in one piece, and I just fell down on the salt and laughed out of relief. Everything was so funny that I couldn't stop laughing. One of the Goodyear public relations men came gasping over the hill and rolled down the other side.

I looked at him and said, "For my next trick, I'll set myself on fire."

He looked at me and then at the car and said, "You know, you're nuts."

I replied, "I'm all right, baby. What's my speed?"

In a few minutes the rest of the group would arrive and I knew that I would have to have something to tell the press. I had to keep Art Arfons off my back; if he thought the car was damaged beyond repair, he would be right back here to run. Anyway, when the newsmen arrived, I said, "It's not damaged badly. We're going to take it over to the air force base and get it ready to run faster."

At that point my sponsors went into a state of shock.

Joe Petrali and his men arrived en masse. Everybody was red faced and scared and out of breath, and I felt really sorry for them. Joe shouted the speed from the top of the dike. "Craig, you went 539 on the second run. You've set a record average of 526.28. Thank God you're here to see it."

A little later, Ted Gillette, the ambulance driver, and his crew dashed over the hill (about 30 minutes had gone by since the crash because they had gotten stuck in the shallow lake — which I thought was a neat trick and, like everything else, pretty funny). Ted had two state patrolmen with him, and they were all in a complete panic. They immediately tackled me and wrestled me to the ground. The doctor was waving a hypodermic needle full of sedatives around and one of the patrolmen pulled out his knife and started slashing the laces of my boots. Right there I got my first injury from the wreck. "You cut me," I screamed. They carried me struggling to the ambulance and switched the siren on. The ambulance was bouncing around over the salt, and the doctor was still waving this hypo around. I raised myself up and said, "Hey, look, I think that the nervous person around here is you. You'd better give that thing to yourself, or put it back in the bag." The doctor put it away. Then Ted almost wrecked the ambulance, and I said, "Listen, Ted, why don't you turn off the siren and slow down? You're going to kill us all." He was even trying to pass cars on the wrong side of the road. I finally convinced him that I didn't want to go to the hospital. The only place I wanted to go was back to the motel and take a shower.

He slowed down and asked in a disappointed voice, "How about a Band-Aid for your cut leg?"

14.

It's Almost a Relief to Crash

Next morning I sat on the bank and looked at the tail of the *Spirit* sticking out of its briny grave. The car obviously was pretty badly damaged and probably would never run again. The strain on the frame and the body supports alone would have made the car unsafe for faster speeds, but I wanted to be there, nevertheless, to see for myself.

The state roads crew had brought a crane in to try to bring the car out, but they were having a little trouble getting the crane out there. The car had gone down in the deepest part of the water, but a small strip of land extended to within eight or ten feet of the left side of the car. Still, the road crew had to bring a bulldozer into play to push some dirt around in order to build a make-shift road so that the crane could roll right out to the car. They got there by about noon and hooked chains around the rear fender supports.

As the car came out of the water, it was a frightening sight. It was pretty much intact, but there was a large hole in the front of the right wheel fairing and the left axle was smashed in — apparently the battle scars given it by one of the telephone poles. Water was whooshing out of it. It looked as if the men were hauling a dead whale out of the deep.

When they'd swung the car to dry land, I went over and looked at it closely. I could plainly see the marks

made by the two telephone poles—one on the left side
of the nose and the other on the left fender cover. I had
already been out to the Flats earlier to look at the
course, and that, too, was quite a sight. I could see the
marks where the car had left the course and careened,
out of control, for five miles before hitting the poles,
which, incidentally, were reduced to millions of tooth-
picks spreading over about a mile of salt.

Besides the dents and the hole from the poles, the
frame was bent, and the salt water had done a lot of
damage to the instruments and the interior and almost
everything that moved. In short, as I had suspected, it
would be impossible to run the car again.

Then I realized I had overlooked something, so I
went around the car again and again. Suddenly I knew
what it was. The movie camera that had been mounted
in the left fender cover was missing. Apparently it had
come off either in the lake or where the car had hit the
poles.

We went back to the telephone poles and couldn't
find any trace of the camera; so it had to be in the lake.
It was important for us to find the camera, because
Goodyear had planned a movie of the record run. If we
could find the camera, we would have the wildest footage of the wildest ride that anyone would ever see.

I called a friend in Los Angeles who was a diver and
told him the problem. "Don't sweat it, Craig," he said.
"I'll be right up there with a diving suit and all the
gear." It was going to cost us some money to find the
camera. Even after we found it, there was no guarantee
that the film would be any good, but it was worth a try.

The diver arrived the next day and went to work.
The search was a little difficult because we didn't know
where the camera might be. The car had hit the water
in one place, skipped to another, and finally gone to the

bottom. The camera could have been thrown off anywhere. But after a couple of hours' searching, the diver came up with one prize. It wasn't the camera, but it was a welcome sight anyway. He had found the canopy. It was in good shape and fit right in place on the *Spirit*.

Then he went back to the lake. About midafternoon the search ended. He found the camera about 300 yards in front of the place where the car had sunk. It had catapulted forward when the car had hit the water the last time.

I had the camera but didn't know what to do with it; so I called Eastman Kodak in Rochester, New York, and told them the situation. They took the problem in stride and told me to put the camera in a bucket of water, put it on a plane, and get it to them right away. They told me not even to open the camera. Their technicians would handle the whole situation and would decide just how to process the film once it got there. Kodak also asked that we send a sample of the briny water along, so that they could analyze it and better judge what to do.

In fact, Kodak did a great job. The film turned out amazingly well. The whole wild ride, right up to the impact with the telephone pole, was there. That jolt must have broken the camera and jarred it loose. The final crash had merely torn it from its mooring. Al Blanchard of Spotlight Films made a movie from this and other footage, and it was so dramatic and exciting that it was nominated for an Academy Award for documentary films that year. But that's getting too far away from the events that followed the wild ride.

It was almost a relief to crash. The pressure that had built up before the 500 MPH run was greater than any I had ever experienced, and I had just wanted to get the whole thing over. After the crash, I felt relieved. I wouldn't have to run at all—ever. The car had been so badly damaged that we knew it would be foolish to rebuild it. We had just about reached the limit of the J-47 engine and the car was not designed to handle a J-79. But I wouldn't tell anyone, and everyone would think I was still in the running.

What I didn't know for some days was that Roy Van Sikle, project manager for the Shell crew, had told the press—after I had been whisked away on the wild ambulance ride—that I was in a state of shock, and that the *Spirit of America* would never run again. That statement blew my whole strategy. I know it did, because later I asked Art Arfons about it, and he said, "The only way I ever convinced Firestone to let me come back was to tell them that your car was destroyed and Goodyear couldn't defend its record."

So it was just a matter of time before Art would get out and run again. I could do nothing about it and went back to Los Angeles to be with Lee and the kids. We had picked out a lot on Palos Verdes Peninsula overlooking the beach, and I wanted to get things rolling on a new house. I had done some of the designs myself; so I was almost as interested in the house as I was in the race car. As a matter of fact, I think I might have been *more* interested at this stage. I just wanted to get away from racing for a while. I was tired.

I was up at the lot one day, watching the bulldozers clear the property, when Lee came roaring up. She jumped out of the car, ran up, and threw her arms around me. She was crying. "Art just went 536. I heard it on the radio," she sobbed. "You're not going back, are you?"

I stared out across the beach and quietly said, "I can't, honey, I don't have a car."

We went back to the house, and I called Earl Heath at Wendover. Earl told me that Art had averaged 536.71 and had blown a tire just as he left the measured mile on the second run. He was able to get the car under control and had not been injured, although the explosion from the tire had ripped away some of the body panels. The panels could be repaired, Earl told me. And he told me another thing: it was snowing on the Flats. The season was closed. Art had the record.

Not only was the record gone with the snow; a number of financial gains also disappeared. Goodyear and Shell had talked of a motion picture and of a car model to be sold at their retail outlets. Both of these projects immediately dissolved into the air. Who wants to see a movie or buy his kids a model of the world's *second* fastest car? I also lost a lot of money from advertising. Both companies had planned big campaigns for the coming year, but since they now didn't hold the record they certainly weren't going to advertise that fact.

Inevitably, I started to think about the inevitable — going back to the Flats and the faster speeds, the effect they would have on the car, and particularly on me. I got to the point that the new LSR project was all I could think of, and I suppose I was unbearable to live with. Lee and the kids just stayed away from me. When I was at home, I would sit in front of the television set for hours, not even knowing what was on. I tried reading, but every book turned out the same way. Along about page two my mind would start wandering, and first thing I knew, the book had slipped from my lap and was lying on the floor next to the blaring television set.

I knew that I couldn't go on this way; so one day I went over and talked with my dad. I had to confide in someone outside the house, where everyone was too

involved. I told him that dying was all I could think of
and that I was really scared to make another run. The
crumpled bodies of my friends who had been killed in
race car crashes kept parading through my mind. I
couldn't sleep at night, and I had become addicted to
sleeping pills—which didn't work, because I would
usually awake with a start after a bad dream and then
couldn't go back to sleep even with the pills.

Dad suggested that I go to see a psychiatrist, and I
agreed to the idea. Someone must be able to help me, I
thought, and though I didn't know what to expect, I did
know that I couldn't go on as I was much longer. So I
contacted our family doctor, who recommended a psychiatrist in Inglewood.

The first visit was quite an experience. To begin
with, the doctor was more nervous than I had ever
been. I felt like asking him if *he* wanted to lie down
and let me sit at the desk. But I told him of my fears,
and of wanting to overcome them because I was a race
driver and the fears were keeping me from deciding
about going back to the Flats and running still faster.

He agreed that it was a somewhat unusual attitude
for someone in my profession and said that we would
try to get to the bottom of the situation. Well, it was a
start, I suppose.

The trouble was, the sessions dragged on and *on*. I
was spending more time telling the doctor about my
childhood and my bicycle and things like that than
about anything else. Every time I would get around to
asking him questions about my fear, he would say,
"Don't worry, Mr. Breedlove, we will get around to
that one day soon." Well, that might be all right for
him—at $25 an hour—but I had to make a decision
pretty soon, and I didn't have the time or interest to go
through my childhood years one more time.

Finally I said, "Look, Doc, I can't go on with this. I'm as messed up as ever. I still can't sleep at night, and I keep thinking about death all the time. What is it with the fear?"

Then he summed up my situation. He explained about my ego and said that I was in competition with my father and was hostile toward women. What about my fear? Well, he said, that was the only normal thing about me and he didn't think I should disturb it.

That was wonderful. I took my "normal" fear and "abnormal" self out of the office and never went back. But I did get to thinking about what he had said and finally decided the doctor was right. It *was* normal to be afraid of going 500 MPH; so I decided to accept the fear and get back to the problem at hand — Art Arfons.

It didn't take me long to assess the situation. Art had a car that was so powerful that it just bulled its way through the record — even blown tires didn't stop it. And *he* would be able to run it again next year. There was only one answer. I would have to build my own car with a J-79 engine — a car that would be so aerodynamically perfect that it would make Art's car obsolete the minute it hit the Salt Flats.

Bill Newkirk, Goodyear's public relations man in Chicago, called the day after I came to my senses and said that the Museum of Science and Industry in Chicago would like to have the *Spirit of America* as a permanent display. What Goodyear wanted to know was — Would I rebuild the car for show, tour the country with it, and then donate it to the museum?

I said, "You mean you want to tour the *Spirit* — even if we don't have the record?"

Bill said, "Look, Craig, that's the first car to go over 400, and it's the first car to go 500 MPH. Everyone will want to see it."

I was delighted at the prospect and told Goodyear that I would be glad to rebuild the car.

It didn't take too much rebuilding to get the car ready just to *show*. All we had to do was replace a few body panels and straighten some things here and there. The car had been strong and was not damaged too badly visually — the bent frame and broken and twisted engine mounts didn't show. We completed the job in about six weeks and left for a nationwide tour.

After the tour and the ceremony at the museum, I started designing a new car — *Spirit of America–Sonic I*, and it would have a J-79 engine *with* an afterburner. Walt Sheehan used two weeks' vacation helping me with the design — particularly the air intake ducts — and things started to fit together again.

Walt and I, with technical assistance from Art Russell, built a model of the car, which I took to Shell in New York. "I want to go back next season and get that record back for you," I told them. Their answer was a firm, positive no. They had had enough of the LSR and didn't want any part of a new effort.

Then I flew to Akron to see Bob Lane and Vic Holt, who was now president of Goodyear. I explained the program to them and asked if they would be interested in sponsoring half of the new car.

Bob said, "Craig, your proposal looks good but" — and this is where I expected to get the ax; I was surprised when he continued — "I don't know if we want to share half of the sponsorship with another company. We would rather take the whole thing."

I was in again!

I was also smarter. I asked if I could get my own subsponsors. When I told Goodyear that I would display the subsponsors' insignias on the back of the car, and that they would be no larger than 25 percent the size of the Goodyear insignia, the giant tire company approved my proposal, and I left Akron a happy race driver again.

Then it was back to Shell—this time with a different pitch. I told Shell that Goodyear had agreed to pick up the whole package, and they couldn't believe it. What, then, was I doing there, they asked. I said, "Well, I'm going to ask you to bet on a horse that has already won. I've been associated with Shell and have an existing contract, and I'd like to continue with your product. I would like credit card privileges for the vehicles involved in the project and fuel to run the car. If I break the record, I want $35,000."

In the circumstances I wasn't asking much, and certainly I was offering great possibilities for a relatively small outlay. Shell agreed to sponsor the car to that extent.

I was really rolling; so I decided to make two more stops before I went back to Los Angeles. First, I went to Cleveland to see Lamson and Sessions Corporation, a major bolt manufacturer. I had used their product extensively on the first car, and they gave me $2,500 worth of bolts and a contract for $5,000 if I broke the record. Champion Spark Plug Company was next. They were vitally interested in racing and were active in the field. They offered me $5,000 if I held the record past December 31. In that way, they could advertise the LSR. The idea was fine with me, and we signed a contract.

When I went back home, I had four sponsors and another dream. I wanted to get right to work because I only had about six months to build the car—I had to get the record back that year—and I knew that it would take every day of the six months to do it. Of course, things were moving so fast that I didn't have time to think about the long year without the record, and that's the way I wanted it. Again, I would *work* my way through a troubled period.

It was already early in March, 1965, and we didn't have two sticks of metal put together—nothing. We had to move. Goodyear wanted that record back because Firestone was pumping away pretty heavily with the publicity, and it really bugged Goodyear. When the salt was ready, they wanted us ready, too.

We found a shop in the Watts area of Los Angeles and ordered the first material so that we could start. The Goodyear contract had not yet come through, but Bob Lane had advanced me $30,000 to get started. We had settled on a $100,000 budget for the car, and another $34,000 for expenses for operating the car at Bonneville. We had had plenty of experience on the first car; so we expected this budget to be considerably more realistic than the one we had asked for the first time. It was. But there were troubles in store.

When the contract arrived, I was shocked to learn that Goodyear expected to own the car after the runs were over. The terms of the agreement stated that I would have the car for three years after the record but that it then would become the property of the company. I didn't like the idea at first, but after thinking it over for a while, I realized that most of the promotional value of the car would be realized in the first three years of the record. Also, I didn't want to muddy the water at that stage; so I agreed to the terms and signed the contract. From that moment it was the same as it had been on the first car—working seven days a week, 18 to 20 hours a day.

Nye quit his job as a fireman and joined the project full time, and Stan Goldstein became office and project manager. This left me with time to work on designing the steering and brakes and every part that went into the car. A lot of the guys from the first project came back, and we soon had eight men working all the time. There was somebody working around the clock, and I was usually there to supervise. When I did sleep, it was usually in the tiny office. I went home only two or three times a week. It was about a two hour round trip to get home, and I just couldn't afford the time. Before long Lee began bringing me my dinner and spending some evenings at the shop.

It was pretty boring for her. Even when she was at the shop with me, I usually had my nose buried in some blueprints. I wasn't much company, but she stayed there, nevertheless, because it was the only way she could be with me. She had taken the new car decision rather badly. She didn't want me to run again, but she knew I *had* to; so she was in my corner—like it or not. About twice a week she would bring the kids over so they could see how the car was progressing —which pleased me. I didn't have the time to take them anyplace and this way I could at least see them. My kids were staying with Lee and me a lot; so since I was seldom home, Lee often had five kids to watch. I guess she had a 20-hour-a-day job also.

As the weeks rolled by, the strain at the shop became fantastic. Not one of us took a day off in five months, and we were all beginning to get on each other's nerves. Tempers often flared. One night one of the guys just flipped and, in a fit of rage, kicked the back door out of the shop. Then he ran back and kicked in the side of the car in several places. It was just a temper tantrum, but by the time we got him wrestled to the floor, he had set the project back by about two weeks. I just looked at the car and said, "Well, we'll have to fix it," and as tired as we were, we went right to work on it—after firing the culprit who had caused us all the extra work.

However, no sooner had we gotten that damage repaired than the Watts riot broke out. The riot was going on all around my shop, and the night sky was brilliantly illuminated with the burning buildings of the strife-torn area. I could just imagine my whole operation going up in smoke—and with it my dreams of the record.

One of the fellows stood guard on the roof at all times, moving from front to rear to watch for fire bombers. Our cars were parked out in front, but there was no way to move them and get them into the relative safety of the shop; so our rotating watchman also had to keep an eye on the parking lot.

So far as the schedule was concerned, the riots didn't hurt us at all because we were on a 24-hour workday anyway. The only difference was now we couldn't go out even if we wanted to. Everything went fine until the day came when we started to run out of material. Naturally nothing could be delivered; so I called everybody together and asked for a volunteer to drive the parts truck through the battle-scarred streets to bring back materials. The reception wasn't exactly overwhelming, and I could see that the volunteer idea was out. There would have to be some sort of contest; so I asked for suggestions.

Stan Goldstein thought up the idea of a golf tournament. We set up the wildest golf course in the world. There were nine holes—which happened to be tin cans, placed at strategic locations throughout that old barn of a garage. The fellow with the worst score on the nine holes would automatically be the parts runner—and the hero.

We placed cans behind barricades and under stairs

and laid out the course through the worst obstacles we could dream up. It would be a one at a time proposition, with me starting. We looked around and found a section of pipe and a pipe elbow—we had the perfect golf club. The ball? We didn't have too many calls for golf balls; so the search was on again. Nye solved the problem. He went to the front door, looked carefully about, and dashed out to his Triumph sports car. He came back with the round gear shift knob. In a minute the first annual Triumph Open was underway.

There really wasn't any par on the course; so my score could have been very good or very bad—we would just have to wait and see. I putted carefully, lining up every one meticulously. There were distractions, such as the cheering when I missed the hole, or the occasional explosions from down the block, and I was a nervous wreck. But I managed to wind up the nine holes with a sizzling 53, which I thought wasn't too bad, considering the situation.

Nye was next, and he had a 58 (he had eight putted the tough sixth hole, which had to be played through a hole in the bathroom wall). Nye was just about ready to boot Stan Goldstein out of the shop when Stan came up with a record 39. We knew why he had suggested golf (I later found out that he played miniature golf as a hobby). Stan even made a hole in one on the third hole, which was a long shot across the center of the garage and under the *Spirit*. The ball went far to the right, hit a piece of angle iron, and bounced into the can, which was taped sideways to the floor.

A chorus of boos filled the air. If there had been anybody outside with the idea of burning the place down, he would probably have left, convinced that we had all just snapped with the pressure. What would be the purpose in burning a room full of lunatics?

George Klass broke the spell. His 72 will stand in the record books of the Triumph Open as the wingding of all scores. It not only gave him the booby prize of two cans of dog food — we had found them while laying out the course — and a crash helmet, but it made him the parts runner.

George wasn't too happy about the honor, but he was willing. As for the rest of us — well, the whole thing had been just the break and relaxation we had needed. We were happier and more relaxed than we had been for weeks, and we vowed to make the Triumph Open an annual affair. (Some of us have gotten together at a miniature golf course almost every year since to continue the tournament — except now we call it the George Klass Open, in honor of our first real hero.)

Well, George left with the parts order and a shot gun, which one of the fellows had smuggled in during the first night of the riots. Weaving in and out of the police barricades, he miraculously escaped harm. He made three runs, and only once did he have any trouble. That time he had to outrun a band of rioters. Fortunately, they were on foot, and the only damage suffered were a few dents in the truck from rocks and bottles. The building and everything else escaped unscathed.

As Watts simmered, the car neared completion. Everything was pretty much on schedule — everything, that is, but one major item. We had designed the car around a J-79 engine, but after five and one-half months, we still didn't have one. I was starting to get really worried, and then, one day, I got a call from a buddy in Arizona who owned a surplus store. I had called him about three months earlier and told him to give me a call if he ever located an engine. When the phone rang, I almost didn't answer it. We were so busy that we often just let it ring, but for some reason I took that call. The voice on the other end said, "Craig, you still want a J-79 engine?"

I thought it was one of the fellows kidding me and I said, "No we're building this race car to run with a great big rubber band."

The voice said, "No, seriously, I've found one for you at Charlotte Aircraft in North Carolina."

It soon was apparent that he *was* serious; so I changed my tune considerably. I called Charlotte, and they did have one! I think it must have been the only one in the country at that point—we had looked everywhere else. I went to Charlotte to look the engine over and found that it had been sitting outside for about three years and was in pretty bad shape. General Electric had built the engine originally and would have to rebuild it if it was to be of any use to us. The plant in Ontario, California, could do it, *if* I could convince the company to take the project.

A phone call put the project right back where it had been. General Electric was not interested in getting involved in racing in any way and politely said no. Then, on the flight back to Los Angeles, I remembered what Bill Lawler had told me about the Shell-Goodyear relationship and how a large corporation would take notice if I used some corporate leverage. I knew that Goodyear stocked GE appliances at most of their service stores throughout the country; so I called Bob Lane when I got off the plane.

"Bob, I finally found this engine," I said, "but General Electric won't help me with it; so I'm afraid we're not going to make the deadline."

Bob gasped at the thought of Firestone holding the record one day longer than necessary and said, "Oh yeah. We buy $40 million worth of appliances from them each year. I think that might help."

By the time I got to the shop there was a phone message from Bob. It said that I was supposed to call Russell DeYoung, Goodyear's chairman of the board, and give him the facts of the case. I called Mr. DeYoung and told him the whole story.

He said, "Just sit tight, Craig. I'm going to make a phone call."

He called back in about an hour and said, "Gerhart Newman, who is in charge of GE's jet engine division, is flying to Charlotte tomorrow. He and his men will have the engine transported to Ontario, and they'll start work on it immediately."

Such things are simple — if you're chairman of Goodyear!

In about five days I got a call from Gerhart Newman. He said, "Mr. Breedlove, we have your engine in good condition. I thought you might like to see it being reassembled. We will test it, and we would like you to be here for that." What a load that phone call took off my mind.

Walt Sheehan and I went over to Ontario and watched as the technicians put the engine back together. Then they had it hauled down to the test stand, which was snuggled between two 24-inch-thick concrete walls, each about 150 feet long. The engine was mounted in this canal and hooked up to the instruments that would measure the thrust and the rpms. At this side of the mounting stand sat a blockhouse, which held all of the controls and offered a safe vantage point for us, since we looked out through 5-inch-thick glass. At the far end of the concrete canal was a 45-degree exhaust deflector.

It was the first time I had seen a J-79 run at close range. When I had watched Art's practice run, I had been two or three miles away. I hadn't even seen his second run; so when the technicians fired the engine up for the first time, I couldn't believe it. The J-79 made the J-47 sound like a peashooter, and by the time it was up to full power, the concrete walls were swaying back and forth. It was the most impressive display of raw power that I had ever witnessed. Then they lit the afterburner. When a J-79 afterburner lights, there is a series of shock waves, and a reddish blue flame shoots out the back because the velocity of the thrust is well over supersonic speed. It sounds just like the end of the earth.

The ground shook and the walls swayed about 12 inches. I thought the whole place was going to come down around us. Smoke and debris were blown about 200 feet into the air, and, I can tell you, I was *scared*. I thought, "And you're going to strap that thing to your bottom and go across the Salt Flats. They're right—you are nuts."

Anyway, the car went together, and we had just put the final lettering on it when I got a call from Bob Masson of Goodyear. He said, "Craig, I've just been talking to Bob Lane. He's been thinking about all of the photographs of the car that will be taken."

I said, "That's right, Bob, and we've got 'Goodyear' right there in foot and a half letters on each side of the car. It will look good in photos."

"I know," he said, "but Bob is afraid that there will be a lot of photos taken from the rear to show the jet exhaust and all, and there isn't any company identification there. Now, you have to look at it from his point of view, Craig. He's got the public relations to think of, and he can't afford any criticism from his bosses. After all, he's out on the limb for a bundle and he has to account for everything."

I said, "Well, what do you want me to do?"

He paused a few seconds, then said, "Bob wants you to put a company emblem on the tail."

"But I've got the American flag on the tail. What about that?" I asked.

"Bob says there's room for both on the tail," he said.

Well, I guess it was partly because the strain of the whole program had caught up with me and partly because I liked the way the car looked; anyway I said, "Tell him I won't do it. The car is all finished and we agreed on the lettering before, and I won't do it."

Bob Lane is a highly professional public relations man (and now a vice-president with Goodyear) and about as proud and stubborn as I am; so when word got back to him what I had said, he went into orbit.

I got another call from one of the public relations men, and he asked, "Craig, can you tell me your side of the story? Bob is so mad, he's incoherent."

I told him the whole story, and he said, "Well, don't say anything else to upset him, and I'll see if I can smooth it over. By the way, Bob says that ... er, the program is off, so better not do anything at the moment. Wait until you hear from me."

Two days later I got a call from Howard Babcock, another public relations man from Akron, who was at the Los Angeles Airport. "I'll be right over, Craig. I have to talk with you," he said.

For two days I had been sitting in the garage staring at the car and wondering what had happened. Lee had come over several times to try to get me to come home, but I had just sat there and muttered, "I don't understand. I don't understand."

But I *did* understand. My feelings had been hurt. I've always had tremendous pride in everything I've built, and I just couldn't imagine anyone wanting to change anything on the car badly enough to scrub the whole program. And my stubborn nature just wouldn't let me give in.

When Howard arrived, the first thing he said was, "Now look, Craig, you and Bob have to work this thing out because there's just too much at stake. Why don't you call him and tell him that you'll put the emblem on the back of the car. Then everything will be all right."

I said, "I'm not putting the emblem up there with the American flag."

Howard said, "You don't have to put it up there *with* the flag. Just put it somewhere on the back; he doesn't care where."

I looked at the car. The subsponsor emblems were on a white stripe that ran the length of the car. They were near the back; so I supposed there would be room for another emblem back there. I pointed to a spot and said, "How about there?"

Howard said, "Beautiful, now call Bob and apologize."

"What do you mean 'apologize'? I thought that's what he sent you out here for, to apologize to me," I shouted.

Howard held his head and said, "You two are driving me nuts. Now just call and say you'll do it. Don't apologize; just say you'll do it."

"Okay," I said, "but I'm not going to apologize."

Howard stared at the ceiling and said, "Just call, Craig, just call."

I called Bob, and we were friends again.

The painter lettered the emblem on the back, and next day Bob Stamm, the company photographer, took the photos of the car that would go in the press kit. Howard waited for the prints and mailed a set, air express, to Akron. The press conference, set for the next day, at the Ambassador Hotel, was a huge success.

The car was a gem. It was larger than the first car, and it had four wheels—no more motorcycle controversy over this one. It sat there in its glistening blue splendor with a large 'Goodyear' on each side at the front. In the back were the emblems of the other sponsors. Right in front of the exhaust opening was a freshly-lettered "Goodyear"—framed by the official company diamond.

After the press conference, Howard called me over and said, "Craig, uh, there's something I want to say."

I looked at him suspiciously and said, "What, Howard?"

He stammered and said, "Well, it's about the lettering. Bob thinks 'Goodyear' on the back is too small."

I turned scarlet and said, "Now, look, Howard . . ."

He interrupted and said, "Hold it, Craig, I've got it all figured out. Just listen. The 'Goodyear' is small because the diamond takes up too much space. Just do away with the diamond. Make the letters as big as the whole diamond border is now. Then everybody will be happy, and I can go home."

I said, "Okay, Howard, but you're going to call Bob and tell him. I won't go that far."

Howard was already running to the phone. "Okay, Craig, that's great. That's great," he called over his shoulder.

15.   The Rocket Car

When I learned that Goodyear was sponsoring Walt Arfons in a rocket car, I was a little upset. I felt that in the *Spirit* they had all the LSR strength that they needed, and it was a blow to my pride to think that they needed a backup car. Wasn't mine enough to fight off Art Arfons's *Green Monster*?

I'm not one to hide my feelings too long; so I called Akron and asked, "What gives?" I was somewhat relieved to learn that the deal with Walt had been made some time before. Goodyear had supplied tires to Walt for his jet drag cars for years, and Bryan Putman, the company's number two public relations man, had told him a long time before that if he ever built his proposed rocket car Goodyear would help him. Walt's contract offered him a flat $25,000 if he broke the record and didn't pay him anything for building the car—with the exception of the rear fender covers and the windshield. Goodyear Aerospace had built those—at fantastic cost. I heard rumors that the windshield alone had cost $15,000. It must have had ground optics! It had taken some pretty expensive aerospace talent to design and fabricate the windshield, and I could see why the space program was costing so much.

The first time I saw the rocket car (it was called the *Wingfoot Express*, as Walt's first car had been named), I nearly broke up. There on the tail, large as life, was the largest "Goodyear" I had ever seen. I knew immediately where the idea had come from!

The car's concept looked pretty good, but the car itself was a little rough; so I wasn't worried. But it did have 15,000 pounds of thrust, and 15,000 pounds was nothing to be sneezed at. The car was shaped somewhat like the first *Spirit;* it looked like a three-wheeled car—except that it actually had two small wheels, close together, in front.

I looked the *Express* over and could tell that it was as strong as a battleship—and probably as heavy. It was absolutely indestructible. Walt later told me the reason for the weight. When he was building the car in his Akron shop, he had a lot of visitors. Each one would ask him what would happen if the car exceeded the sound barrier. He would ponder the question and say, "I don't really know." After each visitor left, the question played on his mind, and he would add a few more steel braces to the car. He finally had to lock his shop door because the floor that supported the *Wingfoot Express* was beginning to sag. If he'd had a couple more visitors, he would have been working on the car in the basement.

The car was to be powered by 15 separate rocket engines, each about three feet long and one foot in diameter. Actually, the rockets were called JATO (jet-assisted takeoff) bottles by the air force, and they had been designed to be attached to military aircraft that needed a boost to take off from extra short runways or jungle landing strips. The solid fuel burned out after only a few seconds, but by then the plane was, everyone hoped, safely airborne. This was the strategy of the rocket car program, too: light the fuse, stand back, and hope the record was in the bag by the time the rockets burned out—not exactly the most scientific approach, but, as I said before, the rockets did represent a lot of power.

Bobby Tatroe, who was driving the car for Walt, was a good guy, but very aggressive and boisterous, and he was going around telling everybody that he was going to fry us alive with the rocket car. He was putting the needle into me pretty far, and I figured that if the car went half as fast as his mouth, I was in trouble.

The day for Bobby's run came, and there were a lot of newsmen there because the car was really unusual. Everyone wanted to see it run. It was bound to be dramatic whether the car broke the record or not. At that stage I figured Bobby was braver than Dick Tracy, and I went over and congratulated him on his courage for getting into that roman candle in the first place. He looked at me from the cockpit and said, "Got a light?" I decided to get out of there. It was bad enough having to share the limelight with Walt and his car without supplying the straight lines for his driver.

Someone gave the signal. Bobby pushed the button or did whatever it is you do to start a rocket car, and the wildest fireworks display I had ever seen began to unfold right there on the Flats. Fire spurted out the back of the car, and clouds of black smoke engulfed everything and everybody. The car was gone. Unfortunately, the rockets fizzled out about halfway through the measured mile, and the speed was only about 385 MPH.

At that point, I'll have to admit that I admired their style, though. Walt, completely undaunted by the miserable showing of the car, proclaimed that they would add *ten* more rockets — five to each side of the car — and come back again. If I hadn't been so involved with my own program, I think I would have gone over and slapped him on the back.

There's one thing I forgot to mention about the rocket car. Each run was so expensive that Walt couldn't afford practice runs; so all of the calculations had to be made on paper from projections made from fairly outdated files of Aerojet General, the company that had supplied the rockets—at a nice round figure of $1,000 each. So each run was costing a bundle. In comparison I was using 60 or so gallons of jet fuel on my runs.

I will say that the *Express* went straight and seemed to handle well enough. The problem was that the car was so heavy that the 15 rocket engines wouldn't move it as fast as Aerojet had said. I didn't know what to expect with the added ten rockets, but I sure was going to be there to see the fireworks.

In Walt's usual speedy manner, the extra rockets were inserted during the night in the sides of the car, pointing back at a 45-degree angle, and the car was ready to run next morning. And in the morning there was Bobby pacing back and forth like a caged animal. He was actually *anxious* to get back in that wild machine.

When they ignited the rockets, I felt like sitting down and writing another "Star Spangled Banner" or something. If Francis Scott Key thought he saw "the rocket's red glare" and "the bombs bursting in air," he should have been at the Flats that morning. I was sure the car was going to start spinning like a top and explode right there on the starting line. Instead, it blasted off down the course with fire coming out all over. Most of the photographers just stood frozen in terror and didn't even click a shutter. I'll bet the editors were furious when the photographers told them they didn't even get a picture of the wildest takeoff in racing history.

Well, the car went straight and true but, unfortunately for Walt, not fast enough. Bobby's average was 470

MPH, but in reaching that speed the rockets had just about burned the car to the ground. Body panels were melted off, and even some of the braces were damaged. The wild and woolly career of the *Wingfoot Express* had ended.

The next day when I wheeled the *Spirit* back on the course, I felt as if I were following a seal act. What could I possibly do to compete with that display? I wasn't even sure a new record would attract much publicity after the run of the rocket car. But I was there to try.

The new *Spirit* stood on the Salt in majestic splendor. Every detail was beautiful. It had a fantastic suspension system with absolutely perfect geometry—I mean, totally correct, so that even when the car went over bumps, there was no wheel toeing—in or out. Under any conditions the wheels maintained perfect, straight traction with the ground.

We got the car out there and simply started running it up and down. After six runs I was up to 500 MPH. The car was a dream. The condition of the salt was poor, but the car seemed to get up and plane through the roughest stuff. The four wheels helped, too. The additional wheel made the car so much easier to handle than the first *Spirit* had been that the improvement was unbelievable. With the three-wheeled car, I had been so busy with the course that I had never really had much time to think about the sensation of speed. Oh, I had known I was going fast and it had been hairy at times, but with this car I could just sit back and steer it and acknowledge the effects of the speed.

Now, for the first time, I could describe how it feels to go 500. It was like being sprayed all over with a million tiny streams of cold water at high pressure. It was invigorating, but the pressure felt strange and I wasn't sure if I was hot or cold. I lost my breath on the acceleration, and only when I reached 500 MPH did it come back. The acceleration, mixed with the funny sensation on my skin, made me a little bit giddy. I felt like giggling.

If I had told anybody that I was out there running the car up and down at 500 MPH and giggling, I would have been carted off in a straight jacket in the back of Ted Gillette's ambulance. It wasn't the straight jacket that worried me so much – it was the ride with Ted. I'd take my chances with the *Spirit* any day!

Anyway, there was little question that we were ready for the record run. We got the car ready for the assault on Art's 536 MPH record on the morning of October 22, 1965. Walt Sheehan calculated the power we would need in order to break the record, and we adjusted the throttle accordingly. I got in the car, went through the check-list, and held my breath while we started the engine. When it was fired up and ready to go, I reached up and lowered the canopy (this one was hinged at the side so I didn't need help, as I had with the first car). I pressed the accelerator to the floor. The car charged off down the black line.

It was an easy, uneventful run—so uneventful, in fact, that I missed the record by 8 MPH. The car had gone only 528, and we couldn't figure it out. Our calculations showed that it should have gone 540 MPH. What had happened?

We ran three more times, and each time the speed was a little under what we had expected. I got a little upset and barked at Walt, "How about getting some power out of this thing? We're not the scenic bus out of Salt Lake City for all tourists, you know!" I felt bad after I said it, but Walt understood that we had a problem and he just buckled down and tried to find what it was *and* how to solve it.

We took the car over to the hangar at Wendover Air Base and tried to solve the case of the missing horsepower. We ran the engine, but the only thing we could find was an occasional deceleration stall that sounded like an explosion. This occurred when the power was cut. For some reason, the compressed, fuel-laden air was occasionally shooting forward on deceleration and exploding. After many adjustments, we seemed to have corrected the problem; so we took the car back to the salt.

When I ran the car again, the air speed indicator pointed to 545 as I left the measured mile. I backed off the throttle, and a fantastic explosion shot fire out of the intake duct, over the cockpit, and about 20 feet in front of the car. The force caved in the whole nose section of the car and split open the top of the canopy. I was sure the entire back of the car had been blown away, but it was "only" another deceleration stall—the grand-daddy of them all. I popped the chute. It held, and the car slowed to the point where I could use the brakes. I had built super-heavy brakes into the new car because of my experience with the other one. They brought the car to a quick stop. The cockpit was much closer to the ground on this car; so I flipped open the cracked canopy and scrambled down to the salt as fast as I could manage. I was surprised to see that the whole racer was still pretty much intact.

There had been a lot of damage, but it was reparable. There were buckled body panels, and the inlet duct had apparently expanded to almost twice its size during the explosion, because it was cracked all around. We hoped the weather would hold while we were working on the car at the air force base. It was going to take a couple of weeks of steady work to get the *Spirit* back in running trim.

16.   Gunfight at the State Line Casino

That night the *Spirit* sat in the hangar at the air force base, following the run that had rivaled the rocket car for fireworks. Was the new car jinx with me again? It seemed that it was the first run with the first car all over again. I had managed to conceal my feelings about not having the record for a whole year, because I was busy building the new car. But now there was no hiding the fact that I was more than a little upset over being second best.

For one thing, I was tired of spending weeks on aerodynamic design and sophisticated systems only to be blown off by Art, who just came up, wheeled his car off the trailer, and ran for the record. Somewhere along the line there had to be a point where the scientific approach took over and the happenstance attack lost out. The *Spirit* was the most advanced LSR car that had ever been built, and there was no reason that it should be relegated to second place.

About the second time through my hit parade of woes, Nye came into the hangar and put his hand on my shoulder. "Well, Champ, it's about time we got started straightening out this big mamma," he said. I didn't look up, and he said, "Here's a little surprise for you."

I looked up and saw Bob Koken, a General Electric engineer, standing with Nye. Bob had been with the program in Ontario, and he told me that GE had asked him to come up and help us out when it was learned we were having trouble with deceleration stalls. He asked me to keep his presence a secret because the company still didn't want too much said about being involved with the racing program. I was so happy to see him that I didn't care what the conditions were. I needed help on that engine!

The crew worked on the buckled and torn body panels, and Bob and I worked on the engine. It took us about six days to straighten the whole mess. We ran the engine time and time again at the hangar, and it seemed to be fine. When we were finished, Bob suggested that we start using the afterburner on the next run. "This way you won't have to push the engine as much, and I don't think you'll have as many problems," he pointed out.

So we lined the car up at the north end of the course for the first afterburner run. I was a bundle of nerves. Again I was about to try something new, and I didn't know what to expect. I had seen the Arfons brothers do it many times and figured that I, too, could hack it; so I plopped into the car like a kid going off a diving board for the first time, knowing the water was cold beneath. You just have to jump in, and, in a few seconds things will be all right. At least that's what you're told.

We lit the engine, and I held the car with the brakes while I checked all of the instruments. Then I slammed the pedal to the floor and lit the burner. And, man, I was gone. I was up to 400 by mile one and felt like yelling, "Yippee, Tex Breedlove rides again!" The ride was fantastic. I could see why Walt and Art had used the burner all along. The burner gets you to the moment of truth in a hurry. I liked that because I wanted to get the record over with.

By the time I got to the measured mile I was going like Jack the Bear. The air speed indicator pointed to 600 MPH. I thought this speed would shut the competition up for a while, but I still leaned back and pressed harder on the accelerator. I knew I couldn't make the car go any faster because of the stop on the pedal, but it gave me a kind of thrill to try. Then I got a terrifying sensation — I began to lose sight of the horizon. At first I thought it was an optical illusion because of the 600 MPH speed. "It must be like the parachute sensation," I told myself. I quickly realized that it wasn't an illusion. The front end of the car was lifting. *I was starting to fly!*

The car veered off the course to the right, and I pulled hard left on the wheel. Nothing happened. The front wheels were off the ground. I slammed the engine off, hit the button for the first chute and felt it tear off. Once again in my haste I had fired it too soon, and the speed had ripped it off. It was like having the same nightmare again. It was all happening once more, and I knew the next step: I would fire the second chute, and it would go. I sat with my thumb frozen over the button for the second chute. Then I pushed it, and, exactly according to the nightmarish script, nothing happened.

I realized I had to keep calm and reason the thing out because I knew that I would not get a second reprieve from the telephone poles and the ten-foot-high dike. "If I touch the brakes lightly, ever so lightly," I reasoned, "maybe the torque from the back wheels and the decreasing velocity will bring the front end down so I can steer again." I moved my boot nearer the brake pedal. It would have to be done gingerly. I touched the brakes easily and let up, and then repeated the operation. It worked. The nose eased down, and I had steering again.

The car now had to be stopped with the beefed-up disc brakes, but that, too, would have to be a delicate maneuver. I couldn't risk having them burn out. There was nothing else. The speed had dropped to 475 MPH; so I lightly pressed the brake pedal, let up so the discs could cool, and then repeated the operation. The car was drifting to the right, but it *was* slowing down. Four hundred. Three hundred fifty. Three hundred. I flashed by mile zero and eased the brakes down again. The car entered the soft salt at about 200 MPH, and I started braking harder. Finally, the car smoked to a stop about two miles past the end of the race course and sank about 8 inches into the soft, briny mud.

This time there was no laughing jag. I was mad, I was tired of having problems, and I wanted the record back. Yet this run had scared me so badly that I knew I must get back in the car as quickly as possible or I might never run again. I'd heard how if, when you are thrown by a horse, you don't get right back on, you may be afraid of horses for the rest of your life. Well, I hadn't been thrown by the *Spirit*, but it had done everything else to me. I had to get right back in it.

It wasn't as easy as I thought, though. The brakes had stopped the car effectively, but they had just about melted away in doing it. The discs were fused into the aluminum wheels, generating such heat that the paint had burned off the frame members up to six inches away from the brakes. The centers of the wheels were badly discolored from the heat, and we had to cut the brakes off the wheels with a torch. The brakes were completely ruined. They had turned to molten masses of metal and apparently had just barely hung together. I had backed off at just the right times to let them cool and solidify. Otherwise they would have melted off after their first application.

We started working on the car in the hangar, but it soon became apparent that we would have to take it elsewhere. We just didn't have the equipment to work there; so I called the air national guard in Salt Lake City and asked if they had the tools and machinery necessary to complete the modifications to the *Spirit.* We were going to have to build bigger fins for the front of the car to prevent it from lifting, and the whole body was going to have to be strengthened because all of the panels had buckled again from the tremendous pressure. Fortunately, for us, Colonel Mulder at the air guard told me to bring the car right in.

The air guard really helped. We had the entire run of the facilities and even borrowed some men to help work on the car. It became a major project. We just took over. We spread out body panels all over the hangar, raised the car on the main hoist, and, in general, filled the whole place. Over in a corner; three guardsmen louvered the straightened panels. We thought that louvering would relieve the pressure, strengthen the panels, and eliminate the buckling. It really was some operation – that is, until the general showed up one day. He took one look at the whole mess and went straight into orbit. "What is this?" he bellowed. Colonel Mulder and I stared at him. I certainly couldn't tell the general that I was a hot-rodder and this was my hobby. But I figured that if I didn't come up with something fast we were all going to Leavenworth for using government property and personnel.

I walked up to the general and said, "Sir, Colonel Mulder has been kind enough to let us use this *empty* hangar and has agreed to let me pay the men for their services and to pay for the equipment we're using to rebuild the *Spirit of America.* It's been sort of an air guard project from the beginning. The California Air

Guard has given us technical assistance; so when we had trouble on the Salt Flats, I knew to come here for the technical know-how I needed."

The general unpuffed a little and said, "Well, I guess if these men are off duty and *you* are paying them, and since the air guard has helped with this project before, it's all right. Get back to work, men."

The colonel let out a sigh of relief and work resumed. I hoped Goodyear would pick up the tab, and consoled myself with the thought that, if not, the bill wouldn't come in for quite a while anyway. I invited the general out to the Flats to watch the run, and I think he would have come if it hadn't been for a trip to the Pentagon that he couldn't get out of. When we returned to the Flats, Colonel Mulder and some of his men were with us. The general told him to go!

We returned with the car after eight days of hard work. I was tired and wanted to be alone; so I went for a walk. I was walking on a dusty street behind the State Line Casino when I came face to face with Art Arfons, who had returned to the Flats that day. He, too, had wanted to be alone. We looked at each other and smiled. It was the first time we had seen each other since he broke the record the first time, and we had both anticipated the moment. In the background the giant cowboy sign at the casino flashed on and off. The western setting completely surrounded us. It was almost as if the two gunfighters had met in the street at sundown, when one of them should already have been out of town. Hollywood would have called it "Gunfight at the State Line Casino."

Art kicked his cowboy boot in the dust and spoke first. "Now that you've got your car straightened out, Craig, I guess you'll break the record again."

If I had had a gun belt, I would have had my thumbs

in it. Instead, my hands were in my jacket pockets. I said, "That's right, Art. I'm going to break the record tomorrow. You were right about the J-79. It really is powerful."

Art said, "Well, what I want to know is if you break my record of 536 and go, say, 546, and I come back and go 556, what are you going to do? Do you intend to come back and keep up this game of Russian roulette, where we go back and forth until one of us gets killed and that's the end of it?"

I looked at him and said, "Yeah, I guess so, Art."

He said, "Okay, that's all I wanted to know," and we both walked away. The stage was set.

Next morning the car looked amazingly good as it sat on the salt, ready for a record run. We had made the necessary modifications and had even touched up the paint that the last run and the repairs had damaged. The new, larger fins had been installed, and the body panels were all louvered. I felt that our flying and panel-buckling problems were over. Another insignia adorned the car — that of the air national guard.

I quickly got into the car and went down the checklist. Again things were moving smoothly. The car was ready. The first run was fast and smooth, and when Joe Petrali handed me the slip of paper at the other end of the course, I was not surprised to see the average: 544 MPH. Now all that lay ahead was the run back.

I adjusted the throttle stop and prepared for my third afterburner run. I blazed through the timing traps at a sizzling 566 MPH and established a new world's land speed record of 555.127 MPH.

That night in the motel we developed the tape from the recorder that would tell us our wheel loading — just how much weight was on each wheel. The loadings would be an indication of the attitude of the car — in other words, was it about to fly or were the new fins doing their job? I was extremely troubled when I saw how light the front end had gotten on the last run. There were only 200 pounds of pressure on each front wheel — pretty light for an 8,000-pound car! I knew that it had not been far from taking off again. I also knew that Art was ready to run as soon as we had used up our time on the Flats.

We had the salt reserved for another week, but I didn't know what to do with it. I certainly didn't want to run the *Spirit* any faster. As a matter of fact, I didn't want to run again at all. I kept thinking of the conversation that Art and I had had in the street and wondered which one of us it would be. We were both too proud ever to quit in second place. I knew Art would go faster than my 555 MPH, and he knew that I would come back after that, light front end or not. Maybe it would be better if we did shoot it out in the street.

17.   Once More for the Women

It was late in October when I established the record at 555 MPH. The season had already lasted longer than usual. There was little chance that it would last much longer, but we still had the salt tied up for seven more days. I intended to use every day of it, and Art was madder than a hornet. He wanted to go.

Art had told the press that we were planning some completely unimportant runs just to keep him off the Flats, hoping that the first snows would close the season and keep him away for another year. He was right. I didn't want to go back out and run that flying machine again if I didn't have to; so I began devising ways to keep the salt. The salt is reserved about a year in advance and in your reserved periods the salt is yours, all *yours*. Nobody can run until you relinquish the salt, or until your time runs out.

So I had time to kill. I called Carroll Shelby and asked if he could let us borrow a Cobra Daytona, the super-fast coupe that had run so well in the Daytona Continental sports car race that year. I told him that I planned to set some endurance records on the salt. He was delighted to supply the car—so long as somebody paid him handsomely for it. The next call was to Bob Lane at Goodyear. I said, "Bob, if we expect to keep the salt, we're going to have to run something. Here's what I have in mind: I can run Shelby's Daytona coupe for 12- and 24-hour endurance records, but it will take about two days to get one ready and up here. In the meantime, what do you think of running Lee in the *Spirit* for the women's land speed record?"

Bob said, "Run Lee in the *Spirit?* Are you kidding?"

I wasn't kidding. The idea hadn't popped into my head until I was talking to Bob, but I wasn't kidding. I hadn't asked Lee, but I knew her well enough to know that she would do it if I phrased it right. Besides, the record was only about 250 MPH, and the *Spirit* almost idled faster than that. The car was silky smooth at 300, and that's all I would want her to go.

"That's right, Bob, we could not only tie up the salt, but we could come off as the fastest husband and wife in the world." The thing was already starting to appeal to me.

It must have appealed to Bob, too, because he said, "Okay, if Lee wants to do it, and you're sure it's safe. I guess you want me to pick up the bill for both runs."

I chuckled and said, "That's right, Bob."

He said, "Okay, you get Lee up there, and I'll have our racing division people talk with Shelby."

I called Lee at home and asked her if she could get a baby sitter for a few days. "Why, do you want me to come up and be with you?" she asked.

I paused for a second. This would have to be worded exactly right. "Yes, honey, I *would* like to have you up here. There are a few things I have to do, and you can help me."

She said she would be glad to do anything I wanted. What was it?

"Well, I would like you to break the women's land speed record."

There was a stony silence at the other end of the line. "You've got to be kidding," she said.

Thirty minutes of fast talking later, she said, "Well, if you think I can do it, I'll try. I guess it would be nice to have some publicity of my own. Maybe it will keep you at home more."

Lee and my dad arrived next morning. The whole thing had been too much for him. He had wanted to come up before, but I had always talked him out of it because I didn't want anyone, not even Lee, who was that close to me around when I was driving. If anything happened to me, I didn't want them to see it. Now, with Lee running, there was no stopping him. He thought the whole family had gone nuts, and I guess he wanted to come up and watch them strap us all in straight jackets and lead us off to a rubber room.

I took Lee out to the *Spirit* and asked her to get in the cockpit. We went over the switches and procedures time and time again. That night at dinner I made her repeat everything to me until I was sure she knew it as well as the contents in her purse. "Tomorrow I'll let you run some 150 to 175 MPH runs. The next day you can up it a little and go for the record when you feel comfortable," I told her.

She did amazingly well in her first run. She went 185 MPH. I aged ten years. While she was in the mile, I was about to go out of my mind. After we saw the chute come out and the car begin to slow, Stan Goldstein came over to me and said, "Look, Champ, you're not going to make it. Calm down. You're about to worry us all to death. You know yourself that she's safe out there."

I said, "I guess you're right. Hey, Stan, do you worry this much when I'm out there?"

He looked at me and said, "Oh, no, you're not that pretty."

Well, when the car stopped, I felt like a proud parent. I bounced over to the car and gave Lee a great big kiss — right on the oxygen mask.

She ran four more times, and I knew she was ready. I told Joe Petrali that we would make the record run next morning.

We set the throttle stop at 60 percent power. Without the afterburner that should give Lee the speed she needed to break the record held by Betty Skelton, who had established it in one of Art Arfons's cars. So there we were again, battling one of the Arfonses. Lee broke the record as easy as pie.

We had a big party that night to celebrate the feat, but I couldn't stay up too late because the Daytona coupe had arrived, and I wanted to start breaking records early next morning on the circular course that had been set up on the Flats. One of the records I expected to break was the 12-hour endurance mark; so I needed a co-driver. The choice was easy. I chose Bobby Tatroe, the wild man from the rocket car. Bobby had been hanging around the Flats because he had nothing else to do after the *Wingfoot Express* had gone up in flames. He was wild about the idea of co-driving the Cobra.

We got out the next morning, and he wanted to take the first two hours. Jumping into the car, he went screaming off on the one-mile circle. Two hours later he slid into the makeshift pit area, and I took over. Neither of us had ever been in the car before, and we were out there running — at about 160 MPH. It was a ball, especially in a spot in the eastern section of the course. The salt was soft and at that point it had broken through to mud. The car would go completely sideways everytime we hit it. We loved that section because it broke the monotony of the whole thing, and we started seeing how far back around the circle we could keep the car sideways after hitting the soft stuff. The crew finally figured we had been inhaling too much carbon monoxide and that it affected our minds.

When the 12-hour period had ended, we had broken 23 world records. We were exhausted because it wasn't easy to sleep during the rest periods, but we had really enjoyed the run.

Then the weather turned bad. It started to rain, and the next day we felt that we could safely leave the Flats. It looked as if the winter snows would soon be there.

Lee and I left the following day for New York, where we were to appear on the television program "To Tell The Truth." As we got off the plane, I was greeted by news that made my whole world collapse. Ben Pope, one of the Goodyear public relations men, was there to meet the flight.

"Craig, I've got some bad news for you," he said. "Art just went 576. The weather cleared for a moment, and he was right there. He rolled the car off the truck and broke the record."

I didn't say a word. I just kept walking.

"He blew another tire," Ben continued. "The car was badly damaged, but he's all right."

"I'm glad he's all right," I said. "Excuse me." I went into the men's room, where I slammed my fist into a metal partition.

The guy behind the partition screamed, "What's wrong? What's wrong?"

The little bit of comic relief brought me back to reality, and I felt better. I went outside and told Lee that we would do the show and return to the Flats tomorrow.

"Craig," she said, "you can't run the *Spirit* again. You know it's going to fly if you go any faster. You can't run it."

"I'll work it out, Lee. I won't take any unnecessary chances, but I have to run again," I said.

When we got to our hotel, a phone message was waiting for me from Bob Lane. I called him back, and he said, "Craig, you don't *have* to go back to the Flats. This whole thing is getting out of hand. You know Art had trouble this time, and you were close to it on your last run. We don't want to force you to go back out there and hurt yourself. As far as I'm concerned, you've fulfilled your obligation to us. You've done a tremendous job for us, and we don't expect you to go back."

I was grateful to Goodyear. But I said, "I know that, Bob, but I *have* to go back. I'm sure I can correct the problems, and if I get the record back, I can keep it because I hear Art's car is damaged so badly that he *can't* come back. I have to go, Bob."

"Well, Craig," he said, "we're behind you if you want to go back, but if you change your mind after you get there and want to step down, you do it with our blessings — and our respect, I might add."

"I really appreciate that, Bob," I said. "I know your concern is a genuine one, but I honestly feel that I can get the record back and do it safely." Part of that statement was true; the rest was pure wishful thinking: I *did* feel that I could get the record back, but I wasn't too sure about the safety angle. I felt that we could modify the front fins some more and maybe make the car stay down through two more runs, but all that didn't really matter. I was driven more than anything else by the fact that Art was out of the show. If I could just get the record, I would hold it — for a long time.

It was as if the other gunfighter had winged me but had run out of shells. The next shot was mine.

I was back on the Flats within 24 hours and was surprised to find that Art was still there with one of his

drag cars. He was running standing quarter-mile
records and just about every fool thing he could think
of to keep the salt. It was his for four more days, and
this time it was *he* who intended to keep it. The weather reports were getting worse and worse. It looked as if
Art was going to beat me at my own game, for there
was little hope that good weather would hold out.
Snow was predicted for the next day, and that would
probably end the season.

Still, I didn't take any chances. We took the *Spirit* to
the air base and began working. If mother nature cast
the dice in our direction, we would pick them up and
go for broke.

Walt Sheehan and Nye and I looked at the car. I said,
"I think if we raise the front end some, it will help."

I reasoned that the low front suspension was the
same as retracting the wheels up into the body. The car
was riding on a cushion of air. With the suspension
lowered, the pressure of the tires against the ground
was reduced, giving the whole car less steering control. I thought that we should raise the front end and
add four more inches onto the trailing edge tab of the
larger front fin, to make the air foil act as a negative
force. The new features would change the pressure
distribution over the entire foil.

After some discussion and eye-ball engineering, everyone agreed that it might work. We made the modifications, and I adjusted the fins to give a 15-degree
angle of incidence, a fantastic down angle. I figured
that if I angled them down as much as three-
thousandths of an inch more, they would stall, we
would lose all the negative lift and the car would fly.
We really would be going on a hope and a prayer.

By the time the car was ready, Art and his crew had
left the Flats. The snow had come, and it looked as if

things were all over for the year. We took the car to the salt and waited, nevertheless. We needed only two runs, and the snow had not yet started to stick. The flakes were large and fluffy, like most first snows of winter. In an hour the sun might shine. It was November 12, 1965. As we sat at the Flats waiting, I thought, "I hope what we did to the car is right." It was not an aerodynamicist talking—just a human being concerned for his life.

18.

That's the Spirit

We sat in the trailer, drinking coffee and waiting. The snow flurries turned to drizzling rain and persisted. It was so cold that nobody even went outside. We just sat there and talked about nothing for three days. We got tired of each other's company and very, very tired of the Salt Flats.

The crew had been there for eight weeks, and they were already talking about the holidays. We were all irritable, and there was no escape from the boredom. The State Line Casino, the railroad station, and Earl Heath's service station became more like home to most of us than anyplace else we could imagine. I had gotten away for two days when I went to New York and for a week in Salt Lake City when we modified the car, but it was all work on those occasions. There had been no diversion.

We got into a parachute controversy one day while sitting in the trailer, and it resulted in our changing the whole system. I guess we were all looking for something to do, and we *had* experienced some problems with the chutes; so the system was a natural target. Moreover, we had both ends of the chute-expert scale working for the project.

I had brought Jack Carter, a dragstrip chute expert,

176

with me from Los Angeles, and Goodyear had sent Fred Neberger, a Ph.D. who had written his thesis on chute designing. The two had worked together to a degree, but they still had their own particular beliefs on how chutes should be made and used. Although I had tried both systems and honestly felt that Jack's was a little more dependable, the Goodyear people had talked me into using Neberger's design since they couldn't imagine a dragstrip chute-maker being able to design and make chutes for anything as fast as the *Spirit.* Fred had designed and developed the Hemisflow chute that was used in the Gemini recovery program.

The Goodyear fellow was probably the leading authority on parachutes in the United States, maybe even in the whole world, but he was in a strange environment, and it was a new ball game for him. He shook his head when he watched Jack Carter working out of the back of his '58 Chevrolet station wagon with a sewing machine older than he was. But Jack's chutes worked every time, and his success baffled the experts.

During the great chute debate and coffee-drinking session, everyone agreed that the main problem with the chutes — aside from the ones that tore off — was pulsation. They would fill with air, deflate, and fill again, giving an uneven slowing action to the car. We had two 90-foot lines on the chutes. I thought that the chutes were too close behind the car and that the lines should be lengthened. Some of the guys disagreed. I think they finally went along with the program just to have something to do. We all agreed on one thing, lengthening the lines wouldn't hurt — so why not try it?

We added 30 feet to each line, but that made the Goodyear chutes fit so tight in the packs that I thought they were going to come out hard. Neberger disagreed. We tried one of Jack's chutes. With the longer line it fit in the chute can better than the Goodyear chute. So I worked out a compromise: we would use the Gemini-type chute as the primary one and Jack's as the backup chute.

Everybody was happy. Ten minutes later when everybody was bored again, somebody said, "What do you think about the brakes?"

I said, "Look, we've got to get out of here. If we sit around much longer, we're going to have the car so messed up it won't run at all. Let's talk to Petrali about the weather forecast."

We went over to Joe's timing shack, and there were the USAC men arguing about the wiring on the timing lights.

"I see you guys are reworking all of your systems, too," I said.

Joe looked up and said, "Yeah, if this weather doesn't break soon, we won't even be able to tell you what day it is with these things, let alone your average speed."

"I know the feeling, Joe. What's the forecast for tomorrow?" I asked.

"More of the same, the weather bureau says."

"Well," I said, "I think I'm going to try a run tomorrow."

Everybody looked up and said in unison, "You're going to do *what*?"

"I'm going to run tomorrow. That's what we're here for, isn't it?" I asked.

It was a while before they were convinced that I was serious about running. While everybody else had been gabbing during the last few days, I had been getting more and more impatient. I knew that the salt, although wet, was not any rougher than it had been before the light snow and drizzling rain. If the wind died down, we would be in good shape. Nobody had ever run in weather that bad, but nobody had ever wanted the record that badly either.

I told the crew and the USAC people that we would try a run in the morning just as soon as wind and rain permitted. If it stopped for even a minute, we would go.

I awoke next morning to the sound of hail on the motel roof and thought, "This ought to be nice to run in." I rolled over to go back to sleep but tossed and turned. Finally I looked at the clock. It was 4:00 A.M., and I got up. I puttered around the room for a while, and Lee woke up.

"What is it, Craig? You're not going to the Flats, are you?" she said.

"I don't know. It's been hailing but it's calm now. I'm going to get dressed anyway," I said.

She was wide awake with this and very concerned. "Are you sure you know what you're doing, with this talk of running in bad weather, and all?" she asked.

"I'm not going to run in bad weather. I'm just going to be ready for the first lull in the bad stuff. When I run there may not be any sunshine and the weather may be cold and damp, but it will be all right to run," I assured her.

We both got dressed and talked for a long time about a lot of things, mostly about the kids and their adjustment to our racing lives. And we were pretty proud of all of them after taking stock. They were good kids. They minded well and were intelligent. Most of all they loved us; so we were proud.

Nye knocked on the door, and we surprised him when we opened it, coats on and ready to go.

"I was up at four," he said, " and it was hailing, but it's not bad now."

I said, "I know," and started down the steps to the car.

The crew had the car ready when we got there; so we sat in the trailer, waiting for daybreak. It came cold and bleak, with no rays of sun, no sign that the weather would get any better. The wind was gusting pretty badly, and it looked as if the hopes for a run were ended.

I walked out of the trailer, and it was blustery. Over at the tiny USAC shack that protected the track stewards from the wind, I asked, "Talked with Joe, yet?"

"He just called and said it was calm in the measured mile," they answered.

That was all the encouragement I needed. I called the crew and told them to get the car ready. If the calm moved this way, we would be ready to go. The skies were black, but it had already started to get less windy, with gusts no more than eight or ten knots.

I got in the car, and I was nervous. I didn't really want to run, I finally admitted to myself, but I knew that if I didn't run today, the place might be under 12 feet of water tomorrow. Then it would be too late.

I waited, and Nye came up to the cockpit. "The wind has died down, Craig. Are you sure you want to go?" he asked.

"I don't have any choice," I replied.

He stepped back from the cockpit and gave the signal to start the engine. I got it fired up, got course clearance from the USAC men, and was ready to go. I moved the engine up into military power—the power necessary just before you light the afterburner—and the car started to slide forward on the tires, despite the fact that I had the brakes locked tightly. I was at the point of lighting the burner—the point where it's all over with and you're gone—when Ben Torres, the USAC steward at our end of the track, started waving his arms, screaming, running in front of the car—literally taking his life in his own hands. I slammed the engine off and threw the canopy open.

"Stop, Craig," he screamed. "Joe just phoned. The wind has picked up to 40 knots in the mile. The signs have blown down and the timing lights are damaged."

The wind hit us in a minute, and I thought it was going to knock over the trailer. We had to take down the striped canvas, leaving the metal frames bare. Then it started to hail and rain—unbelievable. I kicked a tire on the van and headed for the car. Back at the motel I was sure that it was all over for the year. Lee and Nye and I talked it over, and they finally got me out of the fit of depression I was in. They reminded me that the weather had changed back and forth all week and that until the rains and heavy snow really came and the course was completely underwater there was still a chance.

The following morning we went to the Flats. It had again stopped raining. Nye went over to the *Spirit* and starting wiping off the canopy and the windshield. Joe was drying his timing lights. The crew was standing around shivering and grumbling. It looked like a repeat of the past five days.

Joe came down to the place the car was parked and said, "We're ready if the weather cooperates, Craig."

I said, "I guess we are, too, Joe. I'm going to get in the car and wait for the first glimmer of good weather. Then we'll try again."

I got in the car and got my safety harness on. At that instant there was a break in the clouds, I could see a bright orange beam of sunlight way down the course, coming through the jet black sky. In another second there was another one. Suddenly it started, one, two, three, and the whole sky was opening up. It was as if someone was opening a shutter and letting a stream of light come down. It took the whole edge off the blackness that had surrounded us for five days.

Nye ran over and said, "Joe says it's great in the mile." I replied, "Let's get it running."

By the time we had the engine fired up, there must have been a dozen light rays coming down. I checked everything, returned the two-fingered victory sign to Nye, and lit the burner. The *Spirit* was off in a spray of salt water, moving swiftly and surely toward the measured mile. Miles three and four flashed by. I could see the timing lights. The measured mile was bathed in sunshine. It looked as if a giant spotlight was illuminating the whole area. The car was nearing 600 MPH and the front end felt light, but I could steer it. I flashed out of the mile and cut the engine. I waited for the proper time and hit the button for the first chute. It didn't work. I waited one mile, hit the second button, and felt the chute pull. It caught, and the earth seemed to tilt again. I hung from my shoulder harness and seat belt, my goggles pulled away from my face by the force. It was as if some giant had taken hold of the chute and hung the car from a nail. Then the force diminished, everything became level again, and I eased on the brakes. The car came to an easy stop at mile zero.

I had averaged 594 MPH and the record was only one more run away.

Jack Carter's chute had stopped the *Spirit*. When we checked we found that the first one had been packed so tightly in the can that it took Joe's Jeep to pull it out. Fred was shocked at the chute failure but guaranteed me that he could fix the problem. I told the crew to put two of Goodyear's chutes on the car and get ready for the return run.

Walt Sheehan asked how the power had been. "It was perfect, Walt," I said. "Now I want you to give me 610 and not a mile an hour faster. The car seemed to be just skimming when I left the mile; so I don't want to push it any more than I have to."

Walt made some adjustments to the engine, and we set the throttle stop. "That should give you your 610, Craig," he said.

"I hope so. I think it will fly right over Floating Mountain with 620," I answered.

Then we made a second decision. We would pull the car back an additional half-mile and use a five and one-half mile buildup instead of the usual five. The extra half mile would give the car a chance to smooth out at the top end before it reached the measured mile. The salt was smooth for the buildup run; so the strategy was sound.

I got in the car and felt good. I knew that this would be the last run in *Sonic I*. It would never go any faster, because we had reached the point beyond which all of the negative lift in the world wouldn't keep the car on the ground. The J-79 was powerful and the car was streamlined, but we had reached its limit. I figured 610 MPH was it.

When I lit the burner, it was with a feeling of confidence. The sun still shone brightly, and the engine sounded like music. The run was smooth, the acceleration rapid. When I reached the measured mile, the air speed indicator pointed to 600 MPH. The car was running true. As I left the mile, the needle just passed 620 MPH. I figured Walt couldn't have gotten any closer than that.

I had complete control of the car as I cut the engine

and just sat there for a second, enjoying 600 MPH. Then I pressed the button for the chute and felt it catch. Everything was going to be all right. I remembered what Nye had jokingly said to me that morning—"You know it's kind of damp out here. When you finish the run, how about parking the car in the garage so we don't have to get our feet wet?" As the car slowed, I wondered if I could do it. I stepped on the brakes a little harder than usual, and the car slowed quickly to 200. I let the discs cool and then pumped them again. Next, I turned the car to the left, in the direction of the recently reerected striped awning that had served as a garage for two Spirits. The big car slowed down and came around to the left.

The car was down to about 50 MPH as it approached the camp. The crew was going out of their minds. To them I had just conquered the world. Putting that car under the awning was my salute to the finest crew in the world, and they knew it.

They were doing cartwheels and rolling in the rain-soaked salt when I got out of the car. They grabbed me and hoisted me right to their shoulders.

"Hey, wait a minute," I yelled, "we don't have the speed yet."

One of them screamed, "We don't care. Anybody that can park that monster in the garage has to be able to break the record."

When Joe came with the speed, a second cheer went up. I had gone 608.211 on the return run. My average was 600.601 MPH. I *knew* that record would hold. Lee ran over and I grabbed her.

"You're going to quit now. I've got a husband back," she bubbled.

My dad grabbed me and said, "And I've got a son back."

I looked over to Joe and said, "Sorry about running over your wires." He just broke up. He was constantly yelling at everybody for running over the wires with passenger cars.

He said, "That's okay, the season is over, but just wait until next year. I'll put a rule in the book about it." He smiled and grabbed my hand.

And the season *was* over. The skies opened up and deluged the place with water. I remember later walking around with water above my ankles and oil cans floating by. There was no doubt in anybody's mind that it was all over.

I looked at the Spirit, sitting there with its nose sticking out from under the awning, water running back toward the canopy, and I thought, "Well done, my good and trusty steed."

Following the 600 MPH run, I went into the trucking business. My motivation was easily determined. I knew that a great deal of the income to be derived from the *Spirit* would come from displaying the car around the country. The big shows paid well for such attractions. And the car was mine for *three* years only. I knew I had to make as much as I could from it within that time, because after that the car would be whisked off to a museum someplace, as the first car had been.

Now, Goodyear had sponsored the three-wheeled car on a nationwide tour; so I asked them if they planned to do the same thing with the four-wheeled car. When they said yes, I asked if I could supply the transportation. The Seven Santini Brothers of New York had hauled the first car and ended up making more money on the deal than I did—and I had *owned* the car. Goodyear was a little upset with them anyway. For one thing, the Seven Santini Brothers had had to build a special van to haul the car to auto shows and important events across the country—the van was part of the program and was specially constructed to facilitate easy loading and unloading of the car—which was fine except that the truck had *Michelin* tires on it when it showed up for the Goodyear tour!

Whatever the reason, the company said yes to my proposal to haul the car myself. So *I* was in the hauling business. Since I was to be paid commercial rates for each trip, I bought a 40-foot, low-bed moving van. After we'd built ramps inside it to hold the car and installed an electric winch, we were ready to start the Breedlove Trucking Company. At that precise point Goodyear decided not to schedule the car for any appearance after all. There I sat with a 40-foot van. My own schedule was so sparse that it wasn't feasible to hire a truck driver and pay all of the expenses necessary to operate the van. I was really in a jam.

After some discussion, I worked out a compromise with Goodyear. They agreed to fill out my own schedule by sponsoring some appearances at major auto shows and special events. In this way I could at least cover the cost of the van and the modifications. So, inauspiciously, my second nationwide tour began.

This tour wasn't as hectic as the first one had been, because I went mainly to the important events. In fact, there were times when days went by without a public appearance. There weren't too many big events, and I liked the pace much better. Most of the showings were fun, especially events such as the New York Auto Show, which draws about two million people each year.

At the New York show the *Spirit* was placed just inside the main entrance, and I later learned that it was the first time a vehicle of any kind had graced that spot. It was probably the last time, too, because the mobs of people that swarmed around the car finally caused the fire marshals to ask that it be moved. It was near the end of the show, however, so they finally relented and allowed us to keep the car in front of the doors.

After the New York show, it was a round of exciting events — the Daytona 500, the Indianapolis 500, Mardi Gras, the Kentucky Derby, and on and on. I was living exactly the way I had always wanted to—making good money, a part of the glamour of the nation.

Lee, however, was less happy about the situation. She had expected to see me around the house more than usual now that I had broken the record and retired the four-wheeled car. Yet, the work on the van and the tour that followed had taken me away immediately and I hadn't spent too much time at home for almost a year.

I found myself more and more in demand for speaking engagements and personal appearances and I was so wrapped up in the show-biz flavor of the whole thing that I felt I couldn't give up the tour. Realistically, too, the tour was somewhat of a necessity because I knew that one day I would have to give up the car, and when that day came, I would be out of work—and income. I was a little like a baseball pitcher with a sore arm. I could see the end of the gravy train, and I wanted to hang on as long as possible.

Then I began to do a lot of television commercials and those, too, took me away from home. One in particular almost wrecked my marriage. I had taken Lee to Nassau for a week so she could get away from things for a while and relax, and I had promised her that I'd do no business there, despite the fact that it was right at the time of the Nassau Speed Weeks. I had really meant it, and I had even paid our own way—no deals with Goodyear or anything. However, I had left word with an advertising agency in New York, which had contacted me before about doing a soap commercial, that I would be at the Nassau Beach Lodge. We hadn't even stretched out on the beach on the first day before I got a phone message. I was asked to be in New York for the filming of a commercial the next afternoon. Lee absolutely had a fit, but we had to leave that evening. There were no other plane connections that would get us there on time.

But if I was living it up — despite some troubles — one guy was not: Art Arfons. He was back in Akron, working feverishly on the *Green Monster* so it would be ready for a crack at the title the following season.

Art had put dual wheels on the rear of the car to try to overcome some of the tire problems he had been experiencing. The torque of the J-79 was so great that it had caused the body to shift and overload the right rear tire, while the high speeds and increased weight had placed too much strain on all the tires. Art thought that the extra tires on the back might distribute the weight better and eliminate the problem, but when I heard about what he was doing, I knew that my record wasn't in jeopardy because the extra wheels were to be *exposed*. I was confident that they would add so much air drag that the car wouldn't even go as fast as before. Even if the tires held up, I knew the car wouldn't go fast enough. At 200 MPH an additional 200 or 300 pounds doesn't mean too much, but at 600 MPH this same drag is increased to 2,000 or 3,000 pounds. This is just too much extra drag to overcome, and Art was adding that sort of drag with the exposed tires.

Nye and I went up to watch the run the following season, when Art first had trouble with the tires rubbing the fenders. The car did get up to about 540, but the crew had so much trouble that they had to take the car back to Akron and work on it again.

While they were back at Art's shop, they welded a big shovel spoiler — a big air scoop — to the underside of the car to try and help with the torque problem. They hoped the addition of the scoop would keep the car level, but I knew that the scoop could only add more air drag. We didn't even bother going back for the second run, and in one way I'm glad. It turned out to be pretty hairy, and it would have scared the wits out of me.

What happened was that when Art took the car back, he was really ready to pour the coal on. Some of the people there told me that the crew ran the car at 100 percent power with afterburner, and when it started off, it was moving pretty well. But something went wrong as the car approached the mile. Somehow it got up on the right wheels and just hung there for a few seconds— at about 550 MPH! Then the right front of the car dug in, and the *Green Monster* literally rolled down the salt for more than a mile with parts flying about as if the whole machine had exploded. When the car finally came to rest, everyone was sure that Art was dead, but fortunately he escaped with only cuts and bruises and some slight damage to his eyes from the salt, which had been ground into them. The car was a total loss, and that was about it for that particular *Green Monster.*

Art built another car the following year, but he only ran it on dragstrips. As a matter of fact, in 1969 he established the world's quarter-mile record with the car at 267 MPH.

Firestone dropped out of land speed record competition after Art's last crash, and I can't say that I blame them. It is murderously hard on tires. My tires were *18-ply*, and by the time we pumped them up to 250 pounds pressure, they were almost as hard as the old solid rubber tires. But it didn't matter. After the last run my tires looked like old rags. They were still strong, but there were bits of fabric showing everywhere, because the rubber tread was very thin (they had been designed this way on purpose—to dissipate the heat). The forces exerted on the car were so great that the bits of fabric as they ripped off had made dents in the body panels a quarter of an inch deep. The salt thrown off the tires actually sandblasted the body away in places. So, I can understand why anyone would cringe when they saw the punishment a piece of equipment takes at 500 and 600 MPH.

Well, the gunfight was over, but I wouldn't be surprised someday if another one started.

Once Art was no longer a threat, I renewed my acquaintance with Donald Campbell. In 1967 he stopped in Los Angeles to see me. I felt honored. Donald was on his way to Australia to run for the wheel-driven land speed record, which officially still belonged to John Cobb. You see, my record was for jet-propelled cars, and even though it is considered the absolute speed record, there is still a category for "orthodox" cars. Donald spent two days with me, and we talked constantly about the effects of speed and aerodynamics. He hoped to go 400 MPH and break that record. I was pulling for him.

After Donald, there were no contacts. Nobody ran against my record, and I was like a king without a kingdom. There was no point trying to break my own record.

I was about to go out of my mind. I had nothing else to do, so I worked a great deal on the design and plans for a jet-powered boat to break the world's water speed record; but getting a sponsor was another story. When Bob Masson of Goodyear's public relations department approached me on becoming a tire dealer, I practically leaped at the idea. I flew to Akron to discuss the plans for the new service center with Charlie Eaves, who is vice-president of marketing for Goodyear.

While I was waiting for the deal to come through on my tire dealership, I continued working on plans for a jet-powered boat that would go 400 MPH on the water and beat Campbell's water speed record, which was then in the 200s; I went to Houston to talk with the people at Humble Oil, and they were interested in my $100,000 proposal. They said they might put as much as $50,000 into the program if I got an additional sponsor. Things were rolling pretty well. I had constructed a model of the proposed boat—with Art Russell's help—a sleek-looking craft that had lots of horizontal stability built into it to keep it from flipping at high speeds. I was getting excited again.

The problem was, as I got more excited, Lee got more upset. I was again obsessed with building a racing machine, and even though this was a boat it was no different in her mind—she felt I was neglecting her and the kids. My own three children were staying with us quite a bit, and the strain of watching five of them was getting to her.

We were getting nowhere. I felt that I had to turn to the boat and the tire store to keep my mind occupied. I had been on the go constantly since my airplane-building days. I had never been without one crash program or another, and I just couldn't stand the "peace and quiet" of the house. It is easy for me to see why some retired men drop dead about six months after they quit work. Inactivity would kill me, too.

Lee couldn't see this. To her it looked as though I was just trying to stay away from the family and was using the boat as an excuse. We fought a lot over it, and neither of us would give an inch.

I was really fired up about the water record at the time. Donald Campbell was running his *Bluebird* boat on Lake Coniston in England and was doing speeds of well over 250 MPH. He was about to run for the record and would probably retire after he had broken it. Too, he had established the LSR for wheel-driven vehicles on his Australian run, at an average speed of 403.1 MPH. I was really happy for him. So far as the water record was concerned, he had told me that if I wanted to run for the record, he wouldn't mind. But first he wanted to set the record over 300 himself. He felt that it would be the last feather in his cap before he retired to the life of an English country gentleman.

Prospects were looking up. My jet boat and new store were under way, and I was looking around for something else to do, when suddenly tragedy struck.

It began one evening as I sat in the kitchen, eating a sandwich and drinking a glass of milk. The television was turned on in the game room, and I was listening to the commentary. The news I heard crushed me. Donald Campbell had flipped his jet boat on Lake Coniston at 310 MPH. He was dead.

I got up and went outside to the swimming pool and sat there until about two in the morning. It took me several days to get over Donald's death. I thought of our pleasant meetings and everything about him — even the fact that he had shared the same birthdate: March 23. My idol was gone, but I haven't forgotten his many kindnesses.

However, the deal for the tire store, which came through about this time, helped me to recover somewhat. For a start it took me away from all boat plans, and Lee was excited at this development because it meant I would be leading a more normal life. I was going to be a businessman, and that would get me away from racing; she felt it would prolong my life-span considerably. It didn't work out quite as she had hoped, however.

For one thing, I was down at the store site in Torrance constantly. As in everything else, I had to have my nose in every brick and piece of tile that went into the building. It was just like the race car; I had to see it all. I might as well have had a pair of bib overalls on and been right in there slinging mortar with the rest of them, because I was there from daylight to dark, looking over everybody's shoulder. After working hours I studied the plans so I could suggest modifications to the contractor next day. There was no hope for me, Lee felt.

So the second blow came when I informed her that I was also going to be a racing tire distributor for Goodyear. She could see the handwriting on the wall. It would mean taking a tire truck to all the drag races — every weekend — and she knew exactly which one of the employees would drive it — Craig Breedlove, owner.

My one saving grace, in her eyes, was the fact that I was in the tire store all the way. To get the franchise, I had been asked to put up $80,000 for the inventory. I, of course, hadn't had that much, what with the new house and everything, so I had worked out a deal with Goodyear. I had $78,000 coming to me from my contract with the company as a racing consultant, so I had offered them the rest of my contract for the tire dealership. They had accepted. But, as a result, the store actually represented everything I had coming from my racing successes, and I was determined to mind the store — figuratively and literally — pretty closely.

Still, the extent of my financial exposure frightened me, so I hired Dick Clemmens, a Hollywood agent, as my manager to get more personal appearances for myself and the *Spirit*. I only had one year to go with the car, and I figured I had better really make hay while the sun shone. Unfortunately for Lee, Dick did get quite a few dates for me, and even before the store was completed, I had started to travel a lot again.

When the store was finally ready, it was a beautiful place. I not only had tires and tire services but sold appliances (General Electric—you remember the deal with the J-79 and the GE engineers) and auto and speed accessories *and* did minor engine tune-ups. I even had started marketing a line of Craig Breedlove speed equipment. A friend of mine made the stuff, and we split the profit. The store was some operation. I had eight employees, and the grand opening was a gala affair complete with Goodyear vice-presidents and the mayor of Torrance and *everything*.

I hired Bard Rudder, a friend from the race tracks, to manage the store, because I had a heavy travel schedule and had to keep moving on the show tour. I badly needed the money I got from appearances while the tire store was getting started.

It looked as if things were going well; I had the show tour and the store. But I still wasn't happy. I wanted to do some racing of some kind—*any* kind. So I got pretty excited when the idea struck me that the auto manufacturers would gobble up the chance to set records on the Salt Flats with regular production cars. With this plan I first went to Ford and laid out my ideas for their Mustang, but they were lukewarm about the whole thing. It was left at kind of a don't call-us-we'll-call-you stage, so I went to Chevrolet and proposed the same thing for their Camaro. Chevrolet liked the idea and asked that I leave my proposal with them for study. Finally, however, they turned it down after long consideration, although sometime later they hired Smokey Yunick, a race car builder from Daytona Beach who had built many stock cars for them in past years, to build up two Camaros to run at the Salt Flats. He built them, and the cars broke many records. That should have been my break, and I felt I deserved it. After all, Chevrolet had used my idea.

Shortly after Smokey broke the records, I got a call

from American Motors. They asked me if I would be interested in preparing two of their AMXs to run at the Flats. And—they wanted me to drive them. The worm had turned. Now I would have a chance to go out there and blow off that Camaro. The American Motors offer not only gave me a chance to run again; it gave me a goal.

I had six weeks in which to prepare the car. The runs had to be made in that period because the AMX had not yet been introduced to the public, and American Motors needed the record runs to pump up their introductory advertising campaigns. Getting the cars ready meant reworking the suspension and steering systems, so they would handle well at extra-high speeds. I also had to take the engines apart completely and rebuild them. I had to balance all of the parts and make sure everything was perfect inside. And it all had to be done with stock parts because there certainly weren't any speed parts for the AMX at that time, as there had been for the Camaro. Then there were the roll bars and a million little speed gimmicks.

Weather was another consideration. The Flats were too wet. Right after the Camaros had run on the circular course, it had rained, and it clearly might be weeks before it dried out again. So we went to Goodyear's proving grounds in San Angelo, Texas. All we needed was a closed circuit course for an official record, and Goodyear had a five-mile circular course that would be fine for the runs.

It was sweet victory at San Angelo. I averaged 175 MPH with the 390-cubic-inch-engined car, and 160 with the 290 engine. In the process I broke 106 national and international records—including every one the Camaro had set. Oh, yes, there's one other point. Lee went with me as my co-driver. I had convinced her that the pub-

licity would do wonders for her ego, which the house-
wife bit had pretty much shattered. It did help, and for
the next few weeks she was happy again. In 1968 we
even did an ABC network television special together.
It was called "The Racers," and we felt close again.

Following the television special, I put together a
proposal for a new Bonneville streamliner and went to
American Motors. It was to be a wheel-driven car as
opposed to the thrust-driven cars I had been running.
The car would be called the *American Spirit* and was
designed to break the international class B, C, and D
records, using American Motors engines in each category. But if, in the event, the B-class engine should
happen to exceed the unlimited wheel-driven record,
we wouldn't mind that, either.

The company liked the idea, so I came back to the
shop and started the project. It seems that every car I
ever got involved with was a crash-program affair; this
one was no different. We started building the car in
August, which meant there were only about four good
months of weather left at Bonneville, and American
Motors wanted the records before the Chicago auto
show in November. I had to get the job done in three
months, and, as usual, it meant returning to a 20-hour
day.

There was one other complication: a few weeks earlier *Car Craft* magazine had started a contest called
The Javelin Speed Spectacular. It was a program in
which thousands of kids all over America answered
questions about American Motors products and wrote a
brief essay on why they were best qualified to be
among the nine final contestants going to Bonneville.
Car Craft would select the nine finalists, and then we
would have a drawing to separate the group into three
teams of three kids each. Each team would be given a

specially prepared Javelin. They were really fantastic cars, fully equipped with almost every piece of racing hardware imaginable: full race engines, roll bars, suspensions, tires, special paint jobs — everything. Each team would have full liberty to tune their car any way they wished. Then I would drive all of the cars to determine which one was fastest. The kids on the winning team would receive all three cars.

Just six weeks before the Bonneville Nationals, probably the biggest speed meet in the world, I agreed to prepare all three Javelins for the contest. But in addition to the three Javelins and the *American Spirit*, I was also preparing two AMX's to run at the Nationals: one was a supercharged version, and the other was a carbureted prototype vehicle that American Motors was considering as a special car for limited production, similar to Ford's Shelby GT. I was busier than ever.

We finished the Javelins and AMX's in time for the Bonneville Nationals, and they really looked sharp. The real problem, I found out, was getting five cars, plus all of the parts, tools, and equipment required to run them, to the Salt Flats. The three Javelins were loaded on open trailers; two of them were carried on top of the old Sonic I trailer that had been modified earlier when we took the two AMX's to San Angelo, Texas, for the 24-hour runs. The other Javelin was carried on my old dragster trailer, which had to be modified for the heavier vehicle. But we still needed more vehicles. Fortunately for us, the big van that we had been using on tour with the *Spirit of America* was at home due to the lull in the show circuit. So we unloaded the *Spirit* and went to work on the van. Finally, after much cutting and hacking, the two AMX's were snugly secured inside.

Since I also have a 35-foot Freuhauf van pulled by a

55 White tractor that is completely equipped as a portable machine shop and this unit has a 3,000-watt A/C generator mounted just behind the cab, I decided to bring that along, too.

When everything was finally loaded and ready to hit the road, I couldn't believe the incredible sight; it looked like a support unit for one of General Patton's tank divisions. We had two giant tractors pulling two huge vans, one 30-foot lift-gate van pulling two Javelins on a 40-foot flatbed trailer, and a pickup truck pulling the other Javelin on my modified dragster trailer. There were also two station wagons and a new Javelin that American Motors had given me for personal use. As a matter of fact, shortly after that someone in Detroit discovered that I had more cars on loan than Roy Chapin, Chairman of the Board of American Motors.

When we arrived in Wendover, the problems began. The Salt Flats had experienced an unusually severe winter and were still very wet for that time of year, but everything had looked great just before the meet. Some of the water had subsided, and the wind had pushed what remained off the speed course. It had collected in pools at the base of the mountains. Then, two days before speed week was to begin, the wind shifted and the water rose to two-inches deep over the entire course. We couldn't go out on the Flats because of the situation, so I had everyone set up camp at the Wendover Motel. We just sat there, hoping the water would shift before the end of the week.

The Javelins were unloaded, and we drew straws to see which team would get which car. The *Spirit of America* crew and myself helped the teams as much as we could without showing favoritism. Actually I think each crew member secretly had a favorite.

It was the first time in many years that Wendover had looked like the good old days. About a thousand hot rods were tuning and making sneak runs down the highway, while everyone waited and fidgeted and waited. Finally, the meet was called off. We had no choice but to pack up the "tank brigade" and make the long trip home.

We put seals on the hoods of the Javelins so that in case we had another chance to run them that year, the kids could start where they had left off. But the endeavor had been expensive and disappointing, and when we finally got everything unloaded and unpacked and stored, I was well behind schedule with the *American Spirit*.

The *American Spirit* was completed in late October along with six supercharged Bonneville racing engines (two 390 V8s, two 290 V8s, two 183 sixes turbocharged). The engines were beautiful. Barney Navarro, who built the six cylinder engines, got over 700 horsepower on the dyno, and Jim Ward, who had practically handmade everything for the V8s, was very optimistic, even though we hadn't had time to dyno them.

The streamliner was low and small and sleek, and when it was finished and painted the people in Detroit were happy. We held a press conference for the car at the Century Plaza Hotel in Beverly Hills. It was a fabulous success with one exception: Lee's attorney subpoenaed me with divorce papers right in the middle of the affair. I was shocked, embarrassed, hurt, upset, and confused all at the same time. I couldn't believe that such a thing could happen — right in front of my sponsors and the press.

But this was not the time to falter. I apologized to American Motors and tried to smooth things over. We had decided to take the Javelins back to Bonneville in order to finish the contest before the *American Spirit* arrived, so I left early with the kids, and Dick Clemens stayed behind to supervise the final preparation of the streamliner for the long trip to the Salt Flats.

When we got to the Salt, weather conditions were bad, and the course was wet. But at least the one good day, without wind and rain, was enough to get the Javelin contest over with.

The *American Spirit* arrived in the middle of snow, wind, hail, and rain. There was no chance of running that year. To say the least, I was *extremely* disappointed. Yet, I had mixed emotions. I needed some time to regroup and get myself together, and at least the bad weather would buy me one thing: time. We packed up, brought everything back to the shop, and unloaded again. The Javelins had to be shipped to the winners, and the engines and equipment for the streamliner had to be stored.

It was about this time that Dick Clemens dropped the first bomb: he informed me that I was $36,000 in debt from the *American Spirit* program alone. The costs had gotten out of hand because the project was put together in such a short period of time that money was spent before it could be budgeted. But that wasn't Dick's problem now; I would have to make good the money from my own pocket.

Dick left, but not before dropping bomb two: the Goodyear store was in trouble, and the $78,000 from the contract was gone. Still, I thought, I had some money left over from the Texas runs. Somehow, I was determined to make it do.

But I was beginning to get desperate. My divorce problems were getting so bad, with depositions and legal entanglements, I didn't know where to turn. Then one of my attorneys suggested that I move to Las Vegas for a quick divorce and make a property settlement when it was all over. That way, at least things would be settled, and I would be able to get back to work again.

It made sense so I moved to Las Vegas. There I decided to do something constructive while I waited: I began taking flying lessons.

Another reason I had agreed to go to Vegas was Pete Fountain, the great New Orleans musician. Pete had told me that it was a great place to relax and, at the same time, hear some good music and see some great shows. He opened there the first night I got to town, and I saw a lot of him during my first two weeks. Pete is very interested in cars and a little afraid of flying, so he had driven his BMW 507, a sleek German sports car, over to Las Vegas, while the rest of his band had flown.

In the afternoons Pete and I went out in the desert and really ran that car. We drove flat out through the back roads, and for a while it was almost like my El Mirage days again. I'll never forget Pete for helping me over that rough period.

The flying lessons were a gas—just like the Sky Kings all over again, only this time I had a life-size trimmer to play with. Then, shortly after I had enrolled in the Hughes Flight School, I met Buster Smith, who would later become one of my best friends.

Buster was taking flight lessons too, and he also was getting a Las Vegas divorce. One day, as Mark Wiley, our instructor, was going over our flight plans, Buster asked me if I would like to move in with him. He said that he was living in his sister's house by himself and that he would enjoy the company. We seemed to hit it off well, and, besides, I could save money. It sounded like a great idea to me, so Buster and I borrowed Mark's pickup truck after our flight lesson and loaded up my belongings.

It didn't dawn on me until Buster was turning up the driveway toward the most fantastic house I had ever seen that Buster's sister was singer Keely Smith.

Her house was a fantastic pad, complete with pool, mirrored bedrooms, sunken bar, ankle-deep car-pet—even a bomb shelter—and it was right on the fairway of the Desert Inn Country Club. Buster and I had a ball. We took flying lessons every morning, stud-ied by the pool afternoons, and partied at night. We received our divorces about five days apart. Buster graduated from flight school, and I bought an airplane. It seemed like a good idea at the time.

Buster and I became very close, and when the time came to return to Los Angeles, he came along to help me with my business problems.

Buster had been Keely's manager at one time and was very sharp, so when we dug into the bills, things rapidly began to get organized.

A break occurred when I was able to book the streamliner into Clark Marshall's auto show in Seattle. I took the car up there myself to save on costs. But when I arrived at Clark's house in Bellevue (it was January, 1969, and the weather on the trip was ter-rible), I found Buster had been trying to reach me by phone.

I called him and took the third bomb hit: the flood dykes had broken in Torrance, and my entire 15,000-square-foot racing facility had gone four feet under mud and water. Everything was ruined—the six racing engines, the two AMX's, tools, equipment, books, records—everything.

Buster lent me some money to get a crew over to clean up, and two days later, just as they were getting most of the mud out, it flooded again. Buster told me he could handle everything and just to sit tight. I don't think he wanted me to see the damage that had been done.

When Buster arrived in Seattle, he filled me in on the details. We didn't waste any time even then. We took advantage of the bad weather to set a 24-hour record on a snowmobile at Evergreen Speedway just north of town, averaging 86 MPH on a Johnson snowmobile.

That's one of my troubles—perhaps my chief trouble—I can never resist a chance to go fast. In this case, the results were bad. The run put me in bed for three days with an injured back—12 hours on a snowmobile had really pounded me—so I missed part of Clark's show and had to take a cut in my fee. And *that* really hurt.

When we returned from the auto show, Johnson Motors offered me a ride in one of their experimental outboard boats for the World Outboard Championship Race at Lake Havasu, Arizona.

I should have known better—but it *was* a very fast boat, and I certainly needed the money from the ride. Unfortunately, the boat caught a strong gust of wind in practice and flipped. I was thrown out of the boat, and it landed on me, going about 75 MPH. The tie rod between the engines caught me right in the small of the back, and into the hospital I went—again.

Later that spring, American Motors decided it would be far too costly to repair all the flood damage done to their engines and still stand the expense of returning to Bonneville for record runs. So, they said, they were sorry but they were dropping the program. I had no idea where I stood.

20.

Getting Going

I dug out from under the mud and salvaged what I could. I made some money from an occasional personal appearance and the sale of my trucks and my AMX. I also managed to hang onto some personal property, which brought in some income. One way or another, I was able to keep going and to pay off almost all of my personal and business debts.

I took a pretty big step back in December, 1969. I had been invited to appear as a guest on a Los Angeles television show, and when I got there, I found that the other guest was a singer. Well, it turned out that the singer was Tonya Campbell, Donald's widow. It was a pleasant reunion, and I was happy to see that she, too, was on the way back up. She had been a singer before she and Donald were married, and I guess this was her way of overcoming the loneliness.

Tonya and I had dinner that night and talked at great length about our plans for the future. Then I asked her the thing that had been on my mind all evening: "Tonya, what ever happened to the *Bluebird?*"

She told me that it was in the Bristol museum, not too far from London, and that five American drivers — including Dan Gurney — had asked her about getting the car out and running it. She had said in each case, "Absolutely not." It's a magnificent $4 million machine, so I wasn't surprised at the great interest.

My next question was obvious. I said, "Would you consider letting *me* get the car out and running for the wheel-driven record?"

Tonya seemed very excited about doing it, and we made plans to go over and try to get the car out of the museum. I had to save and scrape for an airplane ticket, but I wasn't exactly unused to that, and I got one.

This was to be the perfect start on the long trail back, I thought. Tonya wanted me to drive the car because she said that she was sure Donald would have wanted it that way, especially since the Summers Brothers broke Donald's record with the *Goldenrod*. It now stands at 409 MPH, and I was sure the *Bluebird* could beat that.

However, as usual, there were problems. When I arrived in England, I met with some opposition. The car and, as a matter of fact, the whole concept of land speed racing are so deeply embedded in the English tradition that the idea of an American driving the *Bluebird* didn't sit too well with some of the trustees of the Campbell estate. The project was also complicated because practically the entire British automobile industry is financially involved in the car. But we finally worked out all of the problems, with a lot of help from Tonya, who pointed out to the trustees that Donald had been so fond of me that she was sure he would have wanted me to have the car.

"If the record is to be broken, he would want it done in the *Bluebird* with Craig Breedlove at the wheel," she told them. Finally, everyone agreed, and we removed the car from the museum.

The next step, still in the future, is to bring the car to the United States and get it ready to run. A few modifications need to be made—some tuning and rebuilding—because the car has been sitting idle for a few years. Basically it is superb; it's beautiful and sleek and should go 475 MPH without too much trouble. It will be called *"Bluebird America,"* and near the cockpit, where the driver's name traditionally goes, there will simply be lettered "Campbell-Breedlove."

The project is definitely on the boards, and as soon as I get the necessary sponsors, I'll be out on the Flats with the car to break the record for Donald.

Breaking the sound barrier—at the altitude of the Salt Flats, 4,200 feet, the speed of sound happens to be 720 MPH—is my ultimate goal, and it's something I've had ten years to think about—every single aspect of it. I go to bed almost every night thinking about it and wake up the next morning with the same thought in mind. While I'm eating lunch, I think about different parts and pieces of the car and how they could go together. I have the entire car, from the rivets to every piece of metal and every fin, complete in my mind. It will be the *Spirit of America-Sonic II.* I've got an auto-pilot worked out to help with the stability and a braking system designed that could slow down Superman.

Sonic II will be powered by a hot rod version of the lunar descent engine used by the Apollo astronauts and designed by TRW Inc., except that "my" version doesn't need some of the extreme refinements that made the space version so expensive. Mine will be a bi-propellant engine; in other words, one that uses two agents to supply the energy to the rocket. In this case, it will be nitrogen tetroxide for an oxidizer and unsymmetrical dimethylhydrozine for the basic fuel. The two fuels will ignite on contact and give me 35,000 pound maximum thrust—seven times the power of the first *Spirit* and more than twice the power of the second. The engine will be very small, so I will be able to build a car that is only 36 inches high and 24 inches wide.

The car will cost about $250,000 and will have all of the refinements that I feel will make it capable of going through the sound barrier. I've studied reports of various air force tests on rocket-powered sleds and missiles, including the ground effects well past 1,000 MPH, and I am confident that *Sonic II* will break the sound barrier.

What special conditions will be in operation when man first breaks the sound barrier on land? First, there will be the effect of shock waves reflecting off the ground. I don't anticipate too much of a problem with the shock waves reacting on the top of the car, but, because of its closeness to the ground, the reaction on the bottom of the car may be a different story. Consequently, the bottom of the new *Spirit* must be designed to minimize the effect of any shock waves that do reflect. We can't stop the reflection, but we can minimize the angle at which the waves strike the ground, and we can reduce the resistance that the car will present to them as they bounce back up.

This is one place where the auto-pilot comes in, too. As the car goes trans-sonic, some parts will become supersonic before the total vehicle does. At this point, when the pressure distribution is shifting and the center of pressure is moving forward and creating a destabilizing effect, the auto-pilot will be compensating automatically on the wheel loading. The car will have a series of three small transistorized auto-pilots that will all vote into a computer, which, in turn, will supply the necessary information to the leveling and stabilizing system. The use of three auto-pilots gives the system a tremendous degree of redundancy: if one unit fails, there are still two voting. The run will continue. In the event that all should fail, the entire system would shut down and the chutes would be released automatically.

This brings us to the braking system itself. Parachutes have now been developed to the point where we know exactly how to measure the correct length of tow lines, how big the attachments should be, and exactly how the chutes themselves should be designed. Chutes now have been developed that will slow the car from the very top end of the speed curve, say from 800 to 500 MPH. At 600 MPH an intermediate braking system, featuring two very large speed-board flaps, will take over to slow the car to about 300 MPH. We proved on the second car that power disc brakes can be designed to stop the car through the lower end of the curve. There will be back-ups on all three basic systems in the new car, because I don't intend to fly over banks again. It's too hard on my nerves, and, besides, Chuck Yeager was the first man to *fly* faster than sound; I want to be the first to *drive* faster.

Structurally, we have a tremendous amount of experience from the *Sonic I* car. We know what we're fighting aerodynamically. The only question at this point is the tire design. There are a lot of exciting new fabrics—such as boron filament that is supposed to be stronger than anything currently used—so I don't think the development of a supersonic car is impossible. It might even be possible to run a car on metal wheels without tires. This could be a development angle for the aluminum companies to work on.

But whatever is developed before I'm ready to go, I'm confident that the car will exceed the speed of sound, will be able to handle the reflection of shock waves, will compensate for any instability through the trans-sonic range by auto-pilot, and will have more than adequate power. I'm sure the design is right.

It is going to be a successful program, and I consider breaking the sound barrier on land the last great frontier for man to conquer. Man has gone to the moon, and we have watched him on television; someday soon Americans will watch the live filming—from the cockpit—of man's first supersonic ride in an automobile.

People ask me if I will quit when I break the sound barrier, and I answer with a positive "yes." And I will—so long as I'm not in the middle of a duel with somebody. If that is the case, I might stay around for a while and run again. But I will definitely quit if I'm the first man to go over 1,000 MPH, unless. . . oh, well, let's wait and see what happens.

In the meantime, I'll fill you in a little on our progress to date. Last year, the *American Spirit* dragster that I built for American Motors was taken out of mothballs. The engine and all running gear were removed, and the chassis was dismantled.

A few simple calculations showed me that there was enough room to install a rocket system without having to enlarge the body or relocate the cockpit. We removed the canopy in order to improve the driver's visibility, so the car is now an open-seater. The tubular frame was beefed-up aft to provide enough structural strength to take a rocket thrust of up to 10,000 pounds.

Converting the *American Spirit* into a rocket dragster required a few other modifications as well: The rear axle was changed to a straight beam type with limited suspension; a new aerodynamic steering fin was positioned on the bottom of the nose; and a new dual parachute system was installed for use on the short stopping areas of most dragstrips. I just finished redoing all of the aluminum body panels and painting the car a beautiful hand-rubbed red, white, and gold with DuPont acrylic.

We are still setting up the propulsion system, which is powered by a heat sink version of TRW's Apollo lunar descent engine.

We should have the *American Spirit* rocket dragster finished by March, 1971, and my plan is this: (1) Break the quarter-mile dragstrip record of Art Arfons; (2) Become the first person to exceed 300 MPH in the quarter-mile; (3) Gain experience with the new rocket system.

I am planning an extensive demonstration tour covering key dragstrips throughout the nation. The main purpose for the tour will be to inform the public of my upcoming attempt to set a new world's land speed record—this time on the other side of the sound barrier.

As I was putting the finishing touches to this book, I learned that Gary Gabelich had broken my world's land speed record with a fantastic run of 622.407 MPH in a car called the *Blue Flame*. It was great news, because I had been fortunate enough to spend quite a bit of time with Gary out on the Salt Flats helping him get ready for the run. The triumph of the *Blue Flame*—and it is a triumph—holds out all sorts of exciting new possibilities. Most intriguing of all is the chance to get back out on the Flats in an all new *Spirit of America*. Now, as I recall, that's where I came in.

Craig Breedlove's Speed Records

History of the Mile World's Land Speed Record

CRAIG BREEDLOVE'S SPEED RECORDS

DATE	LOCATION	CLASS	SPEED (MPH)
July, 1954	Saugus Dragstrip	Gas coupe record	103.84
June, 1955	Saugus Dragstrip	Fuel coupe record	116.23
July, 1955	Santa Ana Dragstrip	Fendered coupe record	118.11
August, 1955	Dry Lakes–one mile	"B" coupe record	146.337
August, 1955	Bonneville–one mile	"C" coupe 1st place	152.90
May, 1956	Dry Lakes–one mile	"B" coupe record	148.45
June, 1956	San Fernando Dragstrip	Fuel coupe record	115.96
September, 1958	Bonneville–one mile	"C" coupe 1st place	154.90
June, 1960	Dry Lakes–one mile	"B" coupe record	149.501
August, 1960	Bonneville–one mile	Lakester one way record	233.966
October, 1961	Lions Dragstrip	AA gas dragster	177.31
August, 1963	Bonneville	World's Land Speed Record	405.45
October, 1964	Bonneville	World's Land Speed Record	468.72
October, 1965	Bonneville	World's Land Speed Record	526.28
November, 1965	Bonneville	World's Land Speed Record	555.127
November, 1965	Bonneville	World's Land Speed Record	600.601

CRAIG BREEDLOVE'S SPEED RECORDS (CON'T.)

DATE	LOCATION	RECORDS
November, 1965	Bonneville	Ten-mile oval — Twenty-four National Class C Closed Course records, driving a Shelby Cobra. Average speed for twelve hours was 150.69 MPH.
February, 1968	San Angelo, Texas	Five-mile oval — The following closed course records were set by Breedlove in a 1968 American Motors AMX:

	CLASS "C"	CLASS "B"
American closed car	62	4
American Unlimited	10	4
National open or closed	12	4
National Unlimited		2
International	6	2
TOTALS	90	16

HISTORY OF THE MILE WORLD'S
LAND SPEED RECORD

DATE	DRIVER	CAR	TIME, SECONDS	AVG. MPH
12/18/98	Chasseloup-Laubat	Jeantaud	57.000	39.24
1/17/99	Jeantzy	Jamais Contente Jeantzy	54.000	41.42
1/17/99	Chasseloup-Laubat	Jeantaud	51.500	43.69
1/27/99	Jeantzy	Jamais Contente Jeantzy	44.800	49.40
3/4/99	Chasseloup-Laubat	Jeantaud	38.400	58.25
4/29/99	Jeantzy	Jamais Contente Jeantzy	34.400	65.79
4/13/02	Serpollet	Serpollet	29.800	75.06
8/5/02	W. K. Vanderbilt	Mors	29.400	76.08
11/5/02	H. Fournier	Mors	29.200	76.60
11/17/02	Augieres	Mors	29.000	77.13
3/17/03	Rigolly	Gobron-Brillie	26.800	83.46
11/5/03	A. Duray	Gobron-Brillie	26.400	84.73
1/12/04	Henry Ford	Ford "999"	39.40	91.370
1/22/04	W. K. Vanderbilt	Mercedes	39.00	92.307
3/31/04	Rigolly	Gobron-Brillie	23.600	94.78
5/12/04	De Caters	Mercedes	23.000	97.26
7/21/04	Rigolly	Gobron-Brillie	21.600	103.56
11/13/04	Victor Hemery	Darracq	21.400	104.53
12/30/04	Barras	Darracq	20.400	109.65
1/24/05	Arthur MacDonald	Napier	34.40	104.65

HISTORY OF THE MILE WORLD'S LAND SPEED RECORD (CON'T.)

DATE	DRIVER	CAR	TIME, SECONDS	AVG. MPH
1/25/05	H. L. Bowden	Mercedes	32.80	109.75
1/26/06	Fred Marriott	Stanley (Steam)	28.20	127.659
11/8/09	Victor Hemery	Benz	17.761 °	125.914
3/16/10	Barney Oldfield	Benz	27.33	131.724
4/23/11	Bob Burman	Benz	25.40	141.732
6/24/14	L. G. Hornsted	Benz	29.01	124.095
2/12/19	Ralph DePalma	Packard	24.02	149.875
4/27/20	Tom Milton	Duesenberg	23.07	156.046
5/17/22	K. Lee Guinness	Sunbeam	27.87	129.171
6/26/24	J. G. Parry-Thomas	Leyland-Thomas	27.75	129.730
7/6/24	Rene Thomas	Delage	25.12	143.312
7/12/24	E. A. D. Eldridge	Fiat	24.675	145.897
9/25/24	Capt. M. Campbell	Sunbeam	24.630	146.163
7/21/25	Capt. M. Campbell	Sunbeam	23.878	150.766
4/27/26	J. G. Parry-Thomas	Thomas Special	21.419	168.075
4/28/26	J. G. Parry-Thomas	Thomas Special	21.099	170.624
2/4/27	Capt. M. Campbell	Napier-Campbell	20.663	174.224
3/29/27	Maj. H. O. D. Seagrave	Sunbeam	17.665	203.790
2/19/28	Capt. M. Campbell	Napier-Campbell	17.395	206.956

°Records above this line for World's Time were made over the flying kilometer, the recognized distance in the early years.

HISTORY OF THE MILE WORLD'S LAND SPEED RECORD (CON'T.)

DATE	DRIVER	CAR	TIME, SECONDS	AVG. MPH
4/22/28	Ray Keech	White Triplex	17.345	207.552
3/11/29	Maj. H. O. D. Seagrave	Irving-Napier	15.56	231.446
2/5/31	Sir Malcolm Campbell	Napier-Campbell	14.65	246.086
2/24/32	Sir Malcolm Campbell	Napier-Campbell	14.175	253.96
2/22/33	Sir Malcolm Campbell	Napier-Campbell	13.23	272.109
3/7/35	Sir Malcolm Campbell	Bluebird Special	13.01	276.82
9/3/35	Sir Malcolm Campbell	Bluebird Special	11.96	301.13
11/19/37	Capt. G. E. T. Eyston	Thunderbolt #1	11.56	311.42
8/27/38	Capt. G. E. T. Eyston	Thunderbolt #1	10.42	345.5
9/15/38	John Cobb	Railton	10.28	350.2
9/16/38	Capt. G. E. T. Eyston	Thunderbolt #1	10.07	357.5
8/23/39	John Cobb	Railton	9.76	368.9
9/16/47	John Cobb	Railton-Mobil Special	9.1325	394.2
8/5/63	Craig Breedlove	Spirit of America	8.8355	407.45
10/2/64	Tom Green	Wingfoot Express	8.7125	413.20
10/5/64	Art Arfons	Green Monster	8.2945	434.02'
10/13/64	Craig Breedlove	Spirit of America	7.6805	468.719
10/15/64	Craig Breedlove	Spirit of America	6.8405	526.277
10/27/64	Art Arfons	Green Monster	6.7075	536.71
11/2/65	Craig Breedlove	Spirit of America– Sonic I	6.485	555.127
11/7/65	Art Arfons	Green Monster	6.244	576.553
11/15/65	Craig Breedlove	Spirit of America– Sonic I	5.994	600.601
10/23/70	Gary Gabelich	Blue Flame	5.784	622.407